D0934136

Returning North with the Spring

UNIVERSITY PRESS OF FLORIDA

Florida A&M University, Tallahassee
Florida Atlantic University, Boca Raton
Florida Gulf Coast University, Ft. Myers
Florida International University, Miami
Florida State University, Tallahassee
New College of Florida, Sarasota
University of Central Florida, Orlando
University of Florida, Gainesville
University of North Florida, Jacksonville
University of South Florida, Tampa
University of West Florida, Pensacola

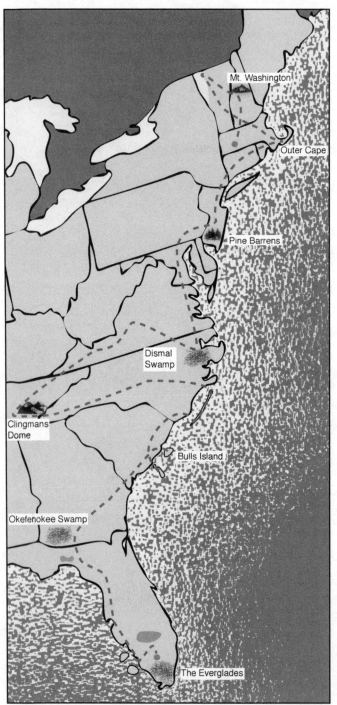

Trip overview

Returning North
with the Spring

JOHN R. HARRIS

University Press of Florida
Gainesville · Tallahassee · Tampa · Boca Raton
Pensacola · Orlando · Miami · Jacksonville · Ft. Myers · Sarasota

Works by Edwin Way Teale are copyrighted by the University of Connecticut
Libraries. Used with permission.

Printed in the United States of America. This book is printed on paper certified
under the standards of the Forestry Stewardship Council (FSC). It is a recycled stock
that contains 30 percent post-consumer waste and is acid free.

This book may be available in an electronic edition.

21 20 19 18 17 16   6 5 4 3 2 1

Library of Congress Control Number 2015952110
ISBN 978-0-8130-6274-7

The University Press of Florida is the scholarly publishing agency for the State
University System of Florida, comprising Florida A&M University, Florida Atlantic
University, Florida Gulf Coast University, Florida International University, Florida
State University, New College of Florida, University of Central Florida, University of
Florida, University of North Florida, University of South Florida, and University of
West Florida.

University Press of Florida
15 Northwest 15th Street
Gainesville, FL 32611-2079
http://www.upf.com

To my parents, for their guidance

For Meade, Anna, Maggie, and especially Susie

Where are the songs of Spring? Ay, where are they?

—JOHN KEATS, "To Autumn"

Contents

Introduction

On a gun-metal gray day in June 1947, naturalist Edwin Way Teale stood high atop the headlands of Cape Cod, his thin tie flapping against his pressed white shirt. He and his wife, Nellie, scanned the waves for signs of life—eiders, storm petrels, herring gulls—but saw only endless sea, beneath which he imagined lay a Lost Atlantis. This couple had spent fifteen weeks pursuing the signs of spring from the Everglades to the Canadian border. The highlights of their excursion included a 6-foot-long rattlesnake, 2,000 glossy ibises, waves of migrating warblers, and a fire that consumed John Burroughs's famous home.

Sixty-five years later to the day, I stand looking out over Cahoons Hollow from my predecessor's elevated perch. In the water below bob dark, cowled silhouettes. Male gray seals, comparatively recent arrivals, now patrol the coastline with the help of federal protection. A few hours later, in a location where Teale knelt to study ant colonies, I stand beside naturalist Robert Finch, who recites a list of other animals that have made a comeback on the Outer Cape: foxes, fishers, turkeys, deer, coyotes, even pine martens. And as we prepare to depart, out of the shadows steps a 200-pound black bear, its cinnamon fur lustrous, its broad stride effortless as it ambles up a hill. The first of its kind to roam this island in more than two centuries, this harbinger of wildness has attracted national media attention by swimming the inlet, foraging the length of the Cape, and now turning for home.

We take for granted that we live in a diminished world, that the bounty our grandparents knew has passed forever from the face of the earth. In fact, many places along the east coast, even locations as seemingly settled as Cape Cod, have grown wilder since the author of North with the Spring described them. I know because I have stood in these places, following in the footsteps of Edwin Way Teale, the most famous American naturalist in the decades between Aldo Leopold and Rachel Carson. Week after week from February through June I stopped where he stopped, compared his lists of flowers, insects, and birds, and bore witness to an ever-warming climate. This book, part field guide, part road trip, documents and celebrates America's east coast wild legacy.

Plotting the Course

At such a time, when you look with dread upon
the winter weeks that lie before you, have you ever
dreamed—in office or kitchen or school—of leaving
winter behind, of meeting spring under far-southern
skies, of following its triumphal pilgrimage up the
map with flowers all the way, with singing birds and
soft air, green grass and trees new-clothed, of coming north with the spring?

EDWIN WAY TEALE, *North with the Spring*

A dozen restless robins balance atop sumac branches on a
south-facing slope not far from my New Hampshire home.
It's late January, midday, and the temperature has peaked at 3
degrees. Jockeying for position among the red-tipped crowns,
the flock appears edgy, and I wonder if this frigid air has re-
kindled their migratory urge, that ancient instinct to join their
brethren in warmer climes. Fifty generations ago robins took
wing: only the heartiest species remained—the junco, chicka-
dee, red-tailed hawk, and downy woodpecker. Today I glimpse
cardinals, bluebirds, titmice, and purple finches, even a stal-
wart mockingbird, hunkered down against harsh New England
squalls. Like these pioneers I too remain in place, impatient
and unsettled in the frozen heart of winter. What would it be
like—just this once—to sever ties that hold me here, to follow

the full tide of the season rising north through 100 days of spring?

Edwin Way Teale set out to answer this question—to trace "firsthand, the long northward flow of the season." Unhappy as a schoolteacher and frustrated as a contributing editor to *Popular Science*, he resigned his post in 1941, determined to follow his own literary inclinations. He plotted a new course, corresponded with colleagues, and waited for a world war to draw to its bloody close. This war cost Edwin and Nellie the life of their only child, David, who died in action in Germany at age nineteen a month before the war's end. This tragedy shattered Edwin's dream and his motivation to write. Their decision to set out in 1947 was thus an enormous gamble, one designed to resurrect hope and to rediscover the equipoise he had lost. The struggle ultimately paid off, for *North with the Spring*, the record of their trip, became a best seller in 1951. Though little remembered today, Teale went on to write eighteen additional volumes and to win a Pulitzer Prize.

"We first smelled smoke as we came creeping down a long green tunnel under overarching trees on a narrow road pockmarked with holes." So begins an adventure in which almost every sentence starts with the pronoun "we," for the author shares his every encounter with Nellie Donovan, his partner throughout the excursion. It was Nellie who urged Edwin to push ahead through the Everglades fire and she who repeatedly rescued her husband from the whirlpool of despair. Physically strong and by nature stoic, Nellie accepted the fact that her husband "was more up and down than I had realized. Oh, if things went well, he was way up in the air. . . . And then if things weren't going too well, [he was] way down in the dumps." Her role in the success of this project and the importance of her companionship thereafter have never been sufficiently recognized.

Edwin acknowledged his dependence on Nellie and called attention to her influence throughout *North with the Spring*.

The volume's index lists twenty-four page references beside her name, and its earliest entry underscores his "added pleasure" when, after twenty-eight years of marriage, she remains "the most congenial person still." An accomplished birder in her own right, Nellie had grown up estranged from her father and forced to look after herself from an early age. Letters passed between the couple during their courtship suggest that she was the more pragmatic as well as the more courageous. Replying to an introductory note sent by Edwin's mother, for example, she responded: "I shall be frank Mrs. Teale—I am afraid of you but not of your criticism. Keep criticizing to any extent for I appreciate it and thank you for it." Such candor, coupled with the steadfast conviction in Edwin's talents, allowed Nellie to play both confidante and guide.

Almost every American looked forward to getting away from home in 1947, after years of suffering and sacrifice. Young people in particular were anxious to throw off the constraints imposed by war. Jack Kerouac, the voice of this new generation, began his *On the Road* adventure during the same year in which Edwin and Nellie set out to follow spring. In many ways the automobile came to symbolize our nation's latent hunger: sleek, shiny, and self-enclosed, cars offered "a speedy, glamorous escape from social conformity." Fifty-four percent of American families owned autos in 1947; by 1960 that number had grown to 77 percent. The federal government paid for the construction of countless superhighways during these intervening years. Sensitive to the times, Edwin Teale fretted that his expedition would seem out of step: "We meet no man-eating bears, encounter no moonshiners or lurid lynching parties." As compared with the "spine-tingling episodes" featured on radio, for television was still in its infancy, he worried that the volume he envisioned would be judged "too quiet for the times."

Rereading *North with the Spring*, with its magical chapter titles—"The Trembling Trees," "Limpkin River," "A Hundred

Miles of Warblers," "The Poisoned Hills"—I found myself slowing down, trusting my senses, finding pleasure in its vivid, vernal portraits. I began to ask myself what had happened to those remote wild places the author meticulously described—most of them unknown to the average American, and many only vaguely delineated on roadway maps. Had development silenced the Florida limpkins? Had time softened or technology transformed the raw, red hillsides of Tennessee's Ducktown desert? Had our insatiable appetite for suburban sprawl eviscerated the Okefenokee Swamp or the New Jersey Pine Barrens? And how had global warming affected these vulnerable landscapes?

As a long-awaited sabbatical approached, I began to dream Teale's dream and to study his early life. *Dune Boy*, an autobiography he published in 1943, portrayed a young Edwin set free to explore the natural world on his grandparents' farm in the sand county region of Indiana. Shy in school and therefore frequently bullied, he chafed under the strict discipline of his Quaker parents and educated himself by reading field guides and taking long summer walks at Lone Oak Farm. Insects became his passion, and Edwin began to experiment with a camera as an adolescent.

Teale became an accomplished photographer and writer, and I spent time studying the negatives he preserved as well as journals from his travels at the archives at the University of Connecticut. A meticulous organizer, he documented each day of their adventure following spring in longhand, filling journals with observations, private musings, and records of every bird they witnessed and every expense they incurred. I had little trouble plotting my route, prioritizing my points of interest, researching what had transpired in the intervening years. The first half of the journey from Florida to Tennessee represented terra incognito for me, and Teale's reports of floating islands, limestone springs, white sand beaches, and trackless swamps made me eager to begin.

Those who travel frequently report that each journey is like an individual person and that, at some point in the excursion, the trip begins to take the traveler. A look at Teale's daily expense ledger underscored these lessons. Breakfasts for the couple averaged less than $2.00, and the combined total for a steak supper outside Orlando, Florida, was $3.40, with a 25-cent tip. The roadside cottages where they typically spent the night rented for $3.50, and gasoline for their black Buick sedan averaged 26 cents a gallon. They splurged 80 cents for an occasional movie (*It's a Wonderful Life* was a favorite), and spent just over $1.00 to have Edwin's suit coats pressed. Twenty cents bought a *Saturday Evening Post* and a pack of chewing gum.

On February 14, Valentine's Day, 2012, I set off with my wife, Susie, sitting beside me. Like my mentor we were surrounded by "maps . . . bird glasses, field guides, and cameras." Snow was in the air that morning, and we slipped across the George Washington Bridge not long after traffic had cleared. The first leg of our journey together was unremarkable, as we stopped for gas somewhere in northern New Jersey. The attendant rang up $53—about what Edwin and Nellie had paid for their entire first week.

The Wildest Place

For miles, we rode slowly along the road, only a foot
or so above the level of a vast cypress slough, the
trees shining silver, the bunched air-plants a feature
of virtually every tree. . . . On the map two non-
existent towns—Trail City and Pinecrest—are shown.
We saw not a single house—once or twice faint road
markings that led off into the pines or palmettos—
nothing more.

EDWIN WAY TEALE, JOURNAL OF *North with the Spring*

On February 21, binoculars in hand, Edwin Teale stepped out
from behind the wheel of his Buick sedan parked along the
shoulder of the Tamiami Trail, a raised ribbon of concrete bisecting the Everglades that had cost a staggering $25,000 per
mile to complete in 1928. Cars whizzed by as he and Nellie focused their attention on a nearby borrow pit, where countless
wading birds fed. They noted herons alighting in the tops of
cypress trees, red-shouldered hawks "with their piercing 'Kee-
You' whistle," and hundreds of American egrets "whose rhyth-
mic wing-beats suggested a waltz." Their long-awaited journey
had begun, and the couple rejoiced in the spectacle of migrating birds: boat-tailed grackles, the "okalee" of redwings, and a
single Everglades kite silhouetted against "a copper-burnished
sunset."

These sojourners were well aware of the poignancy of their pilgrimage. By "leaving everyday responsibilities behind" and gradually drifting north, they were rehearsing a dream shared by millions of Americans, and in their choice of spring, that season of hope, they extolled "belief and optimism . . . where all things seem possible." They also recognized that for thousands like themselves, the joys of slowing down and the excitement of identifying new creatures and meeting new friends would hold only momentary pleasure. Thus, as he drove past houses on the edge of the Everglades, Edwin lamented that they knew nothing of the people inside—"only this we know: troubles, troubles of some kind—money worries, illness, worries over children." Months of immersion in places judged remote, together with Nellie's constant optimism, would be required to lift this veil.

On February 21, 2012, sixty-five years later to the day, I arrive at the Tamiami Trail. The cramped huts and thatched roofs of Seminole Indians bear a striking resemblance to Teale's depictions, and lush green air plants wave from every tree. Recently elevated via bridges and causeways to encourage the flow of water beneath, the Tamiami highway now forms the northeast boundary of Everglades National Park. Therefore, I stop here only briefly, noting a few birds as well as relentless tourist traffic before continuing south to Homestead, where I pick up the former Ingraham highway, a road unavailable to Teale due to heavy rains when he arrived. Parking at the Royal Palm Visitor Center, I head for the Anhinga Trail, a celebrated stretch of boardwalk following Taylor Slough and located almost 50 miles south of where Teale once stood.

A tall woman with close-cropped silver hair and an inviting smile waves to welcome me onto the boardwalk. Anne McCrary Sullivan, the park's resident poet and a birder like Nellie Teale, has expressed an interest in my project and scheduled this location for us to meet. Without hesitation she takes me to her favorite outpost midway along the trail. Here she tells me what

An anhinga perches on its namesake trail in Everglades National Park.
Photo by author.

she witnessed the day she arrived three years earlier: sightseers pointing cameras, egrets gliding out beyond pond apple
trees on the opposite shore, and those theatrical snakebirds,
the anhingas, hissing to one another in sudden alarm. Far out
along the edge of land and water lay a writhing mass of snake
and alligator.

The dark outline of the plated gator churns toward the
slough, its tail thrashing, and wrapped twice around its midsection is an enormous coil of smooth-skinned python. Dark
olive, with fawn-brown stippling, the snake pokes up its head,
its thick muscle searching for another point of anchor. Soon
the pair explodes into the water and disappears beneath the
lilies, a foaming brown wave scattering birds in all directions.

Ten minutes later the reptiles resurface: the python wrapped tightly around the gator's snout. It lifts its head once more, opens its mouth to breathe, and squeezes with greater force. The alligator responds by again submerging its attacker. This time it's nearly twenty minutes before the pair resurfaces, and the gator has managed to get a piece of the snake's thick midsection between its jaws. The eyes of both creatures, now mere slits, suggest neither retreat nor fright.

All afternoon the battle wages. The alligator thrusts up its snout, waiting to feel a pressure subside: the python, in response, rises above the surface and glares. Hour after hour, from slough to shoreline, the struggle continues. By sunset both reptiles are clearly spent, motionless—yet neither appears capable of finding a way apart.

At first light the creatures remain locked in their embrace, exhausted along shore, each awaiting an uncertain end. Then suddenly something lets go. A slip of a coil, the jaw relaxed, and the snake hangs free almost without awareness of its uncoupling. Time suspends them for a frozen moment, and then they separate—moving away from each other faster than Anne imagined possible.

Scenes like this one, memorialized in her poem "Holding On," characterize the new Everglades, a treeless jungle where invasive and voracious predators lie in stealth, threatening everything smaller than adult deer and gradually moving north. According to park wildlife officials, as many as 100,000 Burmese pythons may be lurking in the shallows, and a study conducted in 2011 indicated that 95 percent of the midsized mammals once observable along roadways have disappeared. I spend the remainder of the afternoon pacing this boardwalk, hoping to glimpse a surfacing snake. After countless highway miles, I gradually return to my senses, marveling at the anhinga's gem-blue eyes and basking in the wetland's fecund air. Wading birds, ducks, and tree swallows enter and exit my field of vision. The black-backed carapace of a softshell turtle materializes, and the shadow of a snakebird glides beneath. Emerald-bright dragonflies, coupled in their mating dance, stitch the water's surface. Meanwhile, dozens of tourists saunter past, pause briefly to follow my gaze, and head on toward the parking lot.

Over a campfire that evening, Anne adds to the list of invasive species, citing creatures left out of Teale's comprehensive index. These include Brazilian pepper plants, green iguanas, and walking catfish. Many of these exotics are recent arrivals, products of a poorly regulated pet and horticultural trade. Others like the melaleuca tree, a native of Australia, have been here for more than half a century. Real estate developers desperate to dry out these wetlands in the 1930s hired crop dusters to fill the air with melaleuca seeds. As a result, these trees now cover more than 500,000 acres of southern Florida, where they continue to expand at a rate of 55 acres per day.

Anne's love for this sawgrass landscape is inspired by nostalgia for the African savanna where she once lived. I detect in her voice a sense of loss, a longing for family far away and yet still loved. The silence that hangs between us brings to mind my own absent father, who died of lung cancer two months before my journey began. Our whole family had gathered at Thanksgiving, sensing that the end was near. By then his skin was papery thin, and we lifted his wheelchair up the front steps. His mind seemed ever active, however, and he quizzed me once more about my trip: where I planned to stay, what I hoped to discover, why I needed to sleep in the truck. Three weeks later his lungs gave out.

The drive from North Carolina, where I dropped Susie off to visit family, to Everglades National Park was filled with reminiscing. I had helped my father edit his autobiography, which he dedicated to his grandchildren in the hope that they might understand the arc of his career. In the work he struggled to explain how his father's early death had shaped the remainder of his long life. At age ten he assumed responsibility for his mother and two younger sisters, who remained his closest confidantes. His mother had followed him to college and lived with him during the hectic years of medical school. Like Edwin Teale, my father was exceptionally frugal, ambitious, and never quite satisfied in his accomplishments. He loved people, enjoyed being the center of attention, and yet lived out his final years almost deaf, partially blind, and utterly alone. Susie and I visited his Long Island condominium as often as we could, and twice a year I made a pilgrimage with him to the farmhouse he had purchased in rural Pennsylvania. He'd envisioned this place as a family retreat; however, with each passing year, my brothers and then my mother grew more distant. Every parent's death creates an empty space, one I hoped to fill by following spring.

Anne Sullivan proved an ideal guide, helping me appreciate the size and scope of the Everglades. The vastness of this alien landscape had confounded its earliest promoters, men like Barron Collier who, after falling in love with the state in 1911, spent $17 million over the next decade acquiring more than a million acres, making him Florida's largest landholder. He initiated a series of disastrous drainage projects south of Miami and later won the contract to complete the Tamiami highway. Collier also financed the construction of Everglades City, the proposed hub for his real estate empire. The Teales had spent their third night in this company town, where the Collier Corporation still owned "every store and every business building." Today, only remnants of Collier's failed vision remain—the wide main boulevard flanked by stately palms, the Doric columns that decorate city hall. For the discerning eye, Anne told me, these subtle reminders of private wealth and rapacious development are everywhere evident in Florida's coastal communities.

Only national park designation saved the Everglades from complete desecration. Its hummocks of cypress, mangrove, palmetto, and pine at first glance appear as wild, remote, and impenetrable as when Edwin and Nellie ventured onto the Fish and Wildlife loop road depicted in the chapter epigraph. Pinecrest, the town Teale mentions, is emblematic of the failed dreams of those early entrepreneurs. Home to some 200 gladesmen in the 1920s, this outpost never garnered the luster that its founder James Jaudon envisioned. When Jaudon lost the competition with Collier over the route of the Tamiami, his hope of attracting thousands of tourists to his Chevelier development subsided, and the road to nowhere he had sponsored gradually returned to forest. In 1947 National Park officials, mandated to re-create a "pristine" wilderness within the Everglades, worked to remove the last vestiges of civilization. Today only a handful of tourists venture onto the loop road, which serves as a southern terminus for one of the rare radio-collared female Florida panthers, the most endangered predator on the east coast. Biologists remain divided as to whether inbreeding has pushed this magnificent species past the point of viability.

In *Liquid Land* Ted Levin portrays the true Everglades as "bridled and balkanized by 1,074 miles of canals, 720 miles of levees, 18 major pumping stations, and 250 control structures . . . a computer-controlled watershed." And writers like Bill McKibben and Jennifer Price underscore that the myth of pristine nature as a "place apart" in the twenty-first century rings hollow almost everywhere. My slow drive the next morning along an elevated ribbon of pavement from Royal Palm to Flamingo reinforced the realization that humans dictate what passes for nature in the Everglades. Tourists short on time can even book a helicopter and "experience" these million plus acres in a single afternoon.

At Eco Pond, a man-made reservoir on the way to Flamingo, spindly legged herons teetered in treetops, snow-white egrets covered every low branch, and roseate spoonbills, feathered an ethereal cloud-bank pink, stitched across the shallows at the water's edge. Scores of birdwatchers huddled along the road, and I joined a clump hunched over their spotting scopes. Several looked up and smiled a birder's welcome as I took my place among strangers, most of whom looked to be half my age. We stood together utterly silent, almost breathless in the presence of such stunning beauty. The spoonbills, I later learned, are an indicator species in Florida waters because their nesting success is closely tied to the region's cycle of freshwater fish spawn. Virtually wiped out by 1900, these birds made a gradual comeback only after Everglades National Park was established. Teale's list of birds observed, which totals 202 species, includes no mention of the roseate spoonbill. Spoonbill numbers continue to spike and slump based on total annual rainfall and the volume of freshwater that reaches their breeding territory during early spring. Today 1,000 pairs nest across Florida, and an estimated 6,000 spoonbills attempt to breed along the Texas and Louisiana coast.

The first half of the twentieth century was known to naturalists as the age of extermination. Fashionable women in America and Europe acquired a taste for feathered hats, a craving that quickly required more and more exotic plumes. Milliners were especially keen for pastel colors and for aigrettes, the long, wispy breeding feathers of species like the snowy egret. In response Florida gladesmen began to slaughter huge concentrations of wading birds, wiping out rookeries around Tampa Bay, along the shores of Lake Okeechobee, and finally deep within the Everglades and its Ten Thousand Islands. Skillful hunters could earn as much as $10 for a single perfect plume. Using small caliber rifles to avoid disturbing a nesting colony, gladesmen crept into rookeries and slaughtered every adult bird, leaving behind starving chicks and thus wiping out two generations. In less than a decade the losses were staggering: Frank Chapman in 1886 calculated that more than 5 million birds were being killed each year in the United States to meet the demands of the feather trade. In 1902 when Guy Bradley accepted the position as Monroe County's first game warden, an ounce of feathers was worth more than an ounce of gold.

Bicycling around the campground at Flamingo late in the afternoon, I came upon an abandoned roadway leading to a tree-lined grove. Here a dozen cement slabs marked the site of some former settlement. At first, I suspected I had stumbled upon remnants of the original town, with its ramshackle fishing shanties, makeshift cane mill, and isolated post office. Designated the "End of the World" by its earliest inhabitants, Flamingo was described by naturalist Leverett White Brownell, who visited in 1893, as a godforsaken place where flea powder was the staff of life and soot from smudge pots coated every structure. Guy Bradley, the martyred Audubon marshal murdered while attempting to defend the nearby Oyster Key rookery, resided in Flamingo until 1905. Like Trail City and Pinecrest, this town was dismantled and its residents relocated to make room for the National Park. Later, I discovered that the debris around the campground marks the site of a staff housing complex damaged five decades earlier by Hurricane Donna, the same storm responsible for washing Bradley's grave out to sea.

An hour before sunset I launch my kayak into Florida Bay. Without noticing signs posted a short distance offshore—my attention distracted by a pair of manatees and by half a dozen crocodiles (saurians never mentioned in Teale's journal)—I make my way out to a small wooded island, the closest of several forested keys. Dozens of plume birds perch on branches as I approach, and the smell of guano soon becomes overpowering. Pelicans are the first to raise alarm, followed by a flock of egrets that lift all at the same time and spiral out across the bay. Backing away from the island as quickly as my arms will carry me, I feel that awkward mix of elation and shame that haunts the accidental intruder. From a safe distance I watch as birds, white against a russet sun, slowly return to their roosts.

Only later do I learn that I have trespassed too close to Bradley Key, named in honor of the martyred man.

Thanks to the Audubon Society and the passage of tough New York State laws, plumes fell out of fashion and wading bird numbers gradually began to rebound. In the meantime, Florida land speculators continued to pursue their get rich schemes. While Teale crisscrossed the Tamiami in search of birds, billboards and newspaper ads heralded cheap land and inexpensive building lots. In fact, the appearance of *North with the Spring* in 1951, with its extended focus on Florida's attractive southern coast, may accidentally have aided promoters in their efforts. However, over time, in fits and starts, federal, state, and local entities across Florida bought up and set aside thousands of vulnerable acres rich in biological diversity. This is the other legacy of *North with the Spring*, an inheritance often ignored by those who lament our nation's losses.

Relegated to the periphery of this extensive wilderness, Teale concluded his opening portrait with a panoramic view: "swallows milling in clouds" above the water's surface; "a green haze creeping over the cypress"; "pillars of smoke" against the distant horizon. Able to explore only the fringes of this unique ecosystem, he misinterpreted fire as a destructive force rather than recognizing its value as a natural annual occurrence. Crocodiles, manatees, and mangrove forests remained beyond his purview.

The next morning Anne Sullivan suggests a canoe trip around Nine Mile Pond, a shallow water body whose surface features clumps of periphyton. PVC pipes mark the route, and we soon establish a graceful rhythm. Anne tells me of her other adventures, of stalking a barred owl, catching and releasing a black racer, singing to lure a male alligator to the surface. We hear the bellow of a courting gator, a sound that Anne likens to "low choral thunder." She encourages me to kayak through the maze locals call Hells Bay, and the next morning I put in around eight. Within minutes the bright sun disappears, shrouded by a tunnel of densely packed limbs. The water beneath me turns coffee black, and white PVC pipes at every confluence point the way. Repeatedly, the pathway narrows so drastically that I must ditch the paddle and maneuver forward hand over hand. After an hour of following the man-made signs, I paddle off into an unmarked channel in an attempt to re-create what earlier gladesmen might have experienced. For more than thirty minutes I weave in and out of intersecting canals, snuffing the fecund air, tasting both fear and joy as I search for the slightest clue—a hint of current on the water's surface, a rubbed patch of mangrove bark. No birds appear: the only wild thing I encounter is a tiny gray-green spider ballooning its way between mangroves. Ultimately, feeling both shipwrecked and fully alive, I retrace my route to the last PVC pipe, paddle onward, and before long reach a "chickee," a wooden platform erected on a hummock of dry land at the edge of a lake-sized opening. Here, as I dock, stretch, and eat my lunch, half a dozen ducks, too far away to identify, bob in the morning sun. On my return through the maze, I come across one other couple, who appear to be newlyweds on a honeymoon voyage. In their eyes I can detect a look of marooned delight.

On my final day in the Everglades I return to the Anhinga Trail. Dozens of these strange snakebirds, part heron and part duck, flap their silver-black wings, stretch their doeskin throats, and dilate their blue eyes. Nearby in shallow water dances a reddish egret, or drunken sailor bird, performing its one-of-a-kind ballet, with outstretched wings and dizzy pirouettes. This bizarre behavior I am told is believed to mask the sun's reflection on the water's surface and thereby draw in unsuspecting fish. Above the egret towers a pair of wood storks, Teale's "wood ibis," creatures brought to life from *Where the Wild Things Are*, with their hideous red-rubber heads coupled to beautiful white-feathered bodies with delicate pink feet. Gliding in to feed nearby come the roseate spoonbills, with their lime-green heads, piercing orange eyes, and bizarre paddle-shaped bills. "It is as though an orchid had spread its lovely wings and descended," one early observer wrote.

I wish I could have stayed another week in the Everglades, the wildest, most fragile place I was to experience in all my travels. I would have set out from Flamingo along the 99-mile wilderness waterway to Everglades City, a route that passes beside Cuthbert's famous rookery, a hidden 2-acre sanctuary that once sheltered hundreds of thousands of plume birds and to this day requires navigational charts and competent paddlers. I actually considered the trip while I rounded Bradley Key, but the wind was in my face and the tides were against me. Back in New Hampshire, I talked with a friend who had made the excursion as a college student thirty years earlier. She recalled her sense of being totally lost in shallow limestone for days and, when the journey ended, feeling more alive than she has ever since.

"Things are seldom as they seem" in this wetland, according to Susan Orlean, who followed Seminole orchid growers. In this last remnant of the American frontier, everything is fluid, "always changing . . . washing away . . . merging into each other." The real Everglades remains a realm of subtle gestures and half-glimpsed stirrings accessible only by kayak or canoe. Anne Sullivan has paddled the wilderness waterway on many occasions, and with a colleague she has published a guidebook. Her poem "Reclamation" expresses her strong desire for this place.

I keep coming back to learn from the limestone
reclaiming colors and subtle motions, becoming a place
for deer and butterflies. And me. Mice, too, somewhere,
and snakes that follow them into the garden of hungers.

Unfortunately, federal protection alone no longer guarantees the continued existence of this endangered wilderness. As a sign along the road to Flamingo reads, "Rock Reef Pass: Elevation 3 Feet." More than 60 percent of Everglades National Park

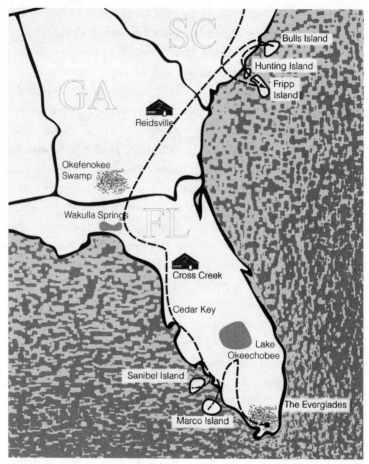

Detail of Florida and Georgia travels.

lies within three feet of mean sea level, and according to Harold Wanless of the University of Miami, the rate of sea-level rise has already increased tenfold since 1930. More recent estimates by the Florida Oceans and Coastal Council predict an increase in sea level along the Gulf coast of between 20 and 40 inches by the end of the century. If the upper limit of this forecast is reached, the vast majority of tidal flats, inland marshes, and freshwater bodies like Eco Pond, the locations where I stood spellbound, will be inundated and lost forever. The mangrove forests that now buffer the coast are also threatened, for if sea level rise occurs rapidly, even these adaptable trees may not be able to keep pace. According to a recent Everglades task force report, species particularly at risk due to climate destabilization include those that are sensitive to changes in temperature and humidity (amphibians), sensitive to salinity (coastal and inland plant communities), or dependent on precise amounts of water (many wading birds). Losing a parent is painful; losing an ecosystem of this magnitude is incomprehensible.

Restoring Our Losses

The flocks ranged from 30 to 70 to several hundred . . . and came in waves minute after minute.
Once 500 birds stretched in one vast struggling line
for miles along the horizon, . . . advancing across
the sky like wave marks on a smooth, sandy beach.
The total count was 2,307 glossy ibis. All the glossy
ibis on the North American continent were concentrated in a single acre . . . on this single bar or island
in Lake Okeechobee.

EDWIN WAY TEALE, JOURNAL OF *North with the Spring*

The key to saving the Everglades, "whose rhythms and pulse
are largely gone," lies with restoring Lake Okeechobee, the
750-square-mile reservoir that forms the ecosystem's liquid
heart. The state of Florida and the federal government have recognized this fact and in recent decades have initiated a number
of massive restoration projects north of Everglades National
Park. Designed to replenish the freshwater required by wading birds and needed to hold back saltwater intrusion, most of
these improvements involve enhancing storage capacity.

The source of several disastrous flooding events between
1920 and 1950, Lake Okeechobee has been hemmed in by massive dikes and constrained by elaborate water control systems
and dredged canals. Teale mentions these engineering marvels

in his journal, for his first experience of a burrowing owl took place "on the great hurricane embankment," and later he and Nellie stood beside a structure that housed "water-level recording instruments." The ever-shifting levels of Okeechobee, only 20 feet at its deepest, helps explain the dramatic difference between the glossy ibis count Teale recorded on March 5, 1947, and the number of these birds my daughter Maggie and I observed on that same March evening sixty-five years later.

As the opening quote illustrates, Teale was deeply moved by the spectacle of long skeins of ibis returning to their roosts. He went to considerable efforts to plan this expedition, awaiting an ideal evening and inviting his companions Rod Chandler, Dick Pough, and Alex Sprunt, all accomplished ornithologists, to help him with the count. And yet, as the sky filled with returning birds, Teale's mind swelled with images of his absent son, "paddling together among bulrushes" on the Saranac River in 1942. His early attempts at joy in March were interrupted by notes of sadness, and although his mood gradually improved through April and May, he would end the expedition still convinced that "man's music is almost unbearable since David's death."

For my part, I had invited each of our three grown daughters to accompany me on a leg of my excursion. We had enjoyed the outdoors together as a family, camping each summer with groups of friends, hiking in the White Mountains, spending afternoons in our backyard woods. Maggie, our youngest, flew in from Oregon, where she was studying to become a deaf interpreter. Sensitive and acutely observant, she asked me how I was doing after my father's funeral. I assured her I was looking forward to our time together, and we worked as a team to prepare breakfast and pack lunches before we set out to meet Dr. Paul Gray, Okeechobee's Audubon coordinator, who had agreed to serve as our guide.

Tall, affable, and energetic, Paul has devoted his life to this body of water, staying on as science coordinator even after his young wife lost her life to breast cancer. He knew and admired the work of Edwin Way Teale and was looking forward to re-enacting the naturalist's bird count. Slipping on ear protectors and taking a seat high above the water, Maggie and I held on tight as Paul maneuvered his airboat around dense swathes of cattails, recently sprayed with herbicides. Although these plants had obstructed Teale's path "down winding trails" to the viewing spot, a dramatic increase in phosphorous levels in the lake has led to their explosive proliferation. Paul pointed to the bright pink eggs of exotic apple snails, a recent invasive that has all but replaced the "snow-white masses" and "pearlike eggs" of the native snails Teale described. The Audubon Society is taking a wait-and-see attitude on whether to begin eradication of this non-native species because researchers have found evidence that the exotics are likely responsible for an increase in limpkin and endangered Everglades kite populations. As if on cue, Maggie points to a slate blue hawk that Paul identifies as an Everglades "snail" kite. After a brief tour of the lake, Paul positions our craft in a dense stand of cattails close to where he believes Teale once anchored. Tucked in beside my daughter as twilight descends, I scan the sky for glossy ibis, breathtakingly beautiful birds with iridescent blue-green wings, a cinnamon neck, and a long downward-curving bill.

Out of the west they come, together with cattle egrets, African arrivals that first appeared on the lake in 1952. Among "the outlandish calling of the limpkins," lines of ibis, sometimes ten, occasionally twenty, crisscross the sky just as Teale had described them. With swift wing beats and long intervals of glide, the ibis circle and settle into their makeshift roosts. Before the light vanishes, we tally 207 of these low-flying silhouettes. Paul quickly explains that glossy ibis no longer concentrate their numbers in a single rookery on King's Bar. Hurricane Francis and Jeanne in 2007 submerged and decimated many of the mature willow groves on this island, and as a consequence, the ibis have shifted their nesting habits, establishing new rookeries

Glossy ibis return to roost on Lake Okeechobee. Photo by author.

on several smaller forested islands. The numbers we witness on this night represent only a small portion of the total glossy ibis population nesting on Lake Okeechobee, a population that Paul assures us is holding its own across Florida. Maggie and I ride home in silence, shivering in response to the night air and the once-in-a-lifetime spectacle we have shared.

In addition to Okeechobee, we board a second boat that week for a tour of the Kissimmee River, one of the Everglades' principal tributaries. The original Kissimmee, a meandering 103-mile shallow, slow gradient stream where Teale had recorded water hyacinths, Florida gallinules, boat-tailed grackles, and an eaglet watching from its nest, was harnessed by the Corps of Engineers during the 1980s to form a canal 56 miles long, 100 feet wide, and 30 feet deep. Decades of hydrological research demonstrated that this channelization was a costly mistake, however, and as a result the Corps, in partnership with the South Florida Water Commission, has begun the most massive restoration project in U.S. history—replacing earlier spoils, dismantling water structures, and attempting to re-create the very wetlands they earlier destroyed. This reclamation effort includes funds to support the Riverwoods Field Laboratory in Lorida. Established as a research and educational facility, its 15-acre campus includes administrative offices, a conference center, boathouse, guest accommodations (where Maggie and I stay), and a residence where Ken Huser, a soft-spoken, deeply tanned Coast Guard Master boat captain, lives with his wife. Ken, the laboratory's caretaker and maintenance man as well as our unofficial tour guide, loves wild Florida, shares stories of alligators and sandhill cranes, and accepts the fact that his residence here is temporary, for at some point the expanded Kissimmee floodplain will inundate and swallow up this entire research facility.

Along with Riverwoods director Louisa Kerwin, Maggie, Ken, and I devote a full day to touring the Kissimmee, comparing the former canal with a section of recently restored river. The contrasts, as one might expect, are staggering. Our boat ride begins along an arrow-straight channel between steep scoured banks, where swallows glide near the water's surface and mockingbirds sing from telephone wires strung high above. Nothing else moves, save for the wake from boats throttled at full speed. However, when we turn off into a restored section of river, we enter a different realm: kingfishers pulse across a surface of lily pads, and alligators slip beneath the waves on either side. A dozen cattle egrets lift and circle beside a bankside willow in which a startled limpkin sounds its catlike yowl. Sleek purple gallinules, strikingly handsome birds, paddle through the vegetation, and at one bend in the twisted floodplain we stop to watch a raccoon tiptoe out on rafts of lilies nonchalantly to pluck up coot eggs. Everywhere we look, the water is alive with fish, turtles, and wading birds. While these first steps have raised expectations, we learn that hundreds of additional acres of wetlands await reclamation and that dozens of retaining ponds, mostly flooded fields, will be required before some semblance of the numbers of birds that once whitened Everglades rookeries might again appear. It remains an open question whether it is realistic to anticipate that these human actions will someday both mitigate the concerns of climate change and mimic the complicated annual cycles of flood and drought upon which life in southern Florida depends.

The most recent proposal to augment water storage north of Lake Okeechobee is the establishment of the Everglades Headwater National Wildlife Refuge in 2012. Designed to protect some 150,000 acres north of the lake, this effort exemplifies the future vision of the U.S. Fish and Wildlife Service, one that relies on partnerships between government agencies and private landholders, most of whom in this case are ranchers. Working for the benefit of wildlife conservation, both parties have enacted easements and cooperative agreements designed to protect, conserve, and restore these important habitats. Much of the protected land will be used for water storage during the rainy season, and once the water is released to replenish Okeechobee, it will become available for cattle ranching.

In addition to counting ibis, Teale traveled north onto a remnant of this Kissimmee prairie in search of "bobbing little burrowing owls, the heavy-billed, long-legged caracara, and the red-topped gray crane." Fifty-four thousand acres of this former ranchland, some improved to support cattle and some left in its original condition, were purchased by the state of Florida in 1997 to preserve the last dry-grass prairie ecosystem in the East. I am fortunate that Paul Gray is available to accompany me, and soon after we arrive at the prairie entrance he points out the hunting shack of Rod Chandler, a famous Okeechobee warden and one of Teale's birding companions. There atop a wooden outpost sits a regal crested caracara, a bird with the outline of a vulture save for its unmistakable falcon beak and golden-plumed head. The male is almost immediately joined by its mate, which flies up from below and settles quickly on a nest in a nearby cabbage palm.

"Most of the roads that access this prairie were constructed by ranchers or military personnel in the 1940s," Paul tells me. "That means we're likely standing in a location where Teale once stood."

One-half mile further down the fence line we notice a pair of sandhill cranes, magnificent long-legged birds with red head-patches and wingspans that exceed those of an adult bald eagle. All around the pair whispers a sea of wiregrass, native prairie vegetation that has reappeared as a result of frequent controlled fires by state and federal wildlife officials. Further on, after several false starts, where we mistake meadowlarks for owls, we finally surprise one of these elfin birds, which flies swiftly from its burrow beside the road to a nearby fencepost. This inquisitive little creature displays a characteristic owl face and bobbing head, a long lean body, and thin yellow legs. Following Teale's lead, I examine its burrow, a 6-inch open-ing in the soft gray sand with an unmistakable apron of talon scratches fanning out from beyond the entrance.

Before departing, Paul reiterates his guarded hope for the future of the Everglades. During his tenure he's witnessed a genuine commitment by all parties regarding the volume of water necessary for Okeechobee to serve as an effective reser-voir. In addition he now believes that the Army Corps of Engi-neers is "beginning to think like ecologists rather than simply engineers." Paul continues to have his doubts that the phos-phorus problem in the lake will be solved during his lifetime, mostly because the sugarcane industry, which relies on phos-phorus as a fertilizer, continues to dump tons of this chemical on fields each year. Excessive phosphorus kills the sawgrass, a native plant that is quickly replaced by cattails, whose thick stands choke out trees and deny wading birds a place to land. Paul ends this tour back in his Lorida office, where he shows me his collection of field guides, many of them first editions by authors like Alexander Sprunt, who, after accompanying Teale on his ibis count, published books for Audubon, helped found the Nature Conservancy, and led the effort to save a remnant of the Kissimmee prairie, after more than 85 percent had been drained and plowed under in the 1970s. I sense that Dr. Paul Gray harbors similar ambitions, and I have no doubt that his tireless activism and commitment to restoration and research will create a significant legacy of its own.

Before leaving Lorida, I want to try my hand at bass fishing in the canal that meanders beside Riverwoods. Ken Huser assures me there are fish to be caught beneath the lily pads. So early one morning I slip into my kayak and begin to toss a lure. On my fourth cast I catch a glimpse of something dark rising to the surface only a few feet from my boat. A snout, two dark knobs, and finally the silhouette of a 10-foot alligator. Instantly I go limp, cradling my reel, resting my paddle, ceasing even to breathe. I feel my "fight or flight" instinct build. Finally, after what seems like an inordinately long pause, the dark apparition disappears. When I take a breath, a reptilian musk lingers in the air as courting cardinals renew their song. I slowly retrieve my lure, paddle without a splash, and silently pull up along the dock. It takes several minutes before I find the courage to slide from my kayak and step onshore.

From this day forth, an instinctive alertness accompanies me whenever I ready my kayak in Florida. Alligators have made a dramatic comeback in the state, so much so that the National Wildlife Service now sponsors an alligator hunt in the Loxahatchee Refuge. I search Teale's journal for his attitude toward alligators and learn that he witnessed a close encounter with an oversized gator during his stay on Bulls Island. Seated in a small rowboat beside William Baldwin, a field biologist,

Teale observed "the largest alligator I had ever seen" appear on Summerhouse Pond while the two men attempted to cross. Even after the shadow of this reptile faded, Teale continued to scan the pond's surface each day with his binoculars. Large predators trigger such a reaction in us, an amalgam of fear and vigilance that John Livingston calls a "participatory state of mind." Such emotions likely date back millions of years, and for some, they form an essential ingredient of an authentic wilderness experience.

In addition to retracing my predecessor's progress across south Florida, I visit several protected parcels that were unavailable to him. The most spectacular of these is Corkscrew Swamp Sanctuary, a 10,000-acre wildlife preserve located 16 miles northeast of Naples. Roger Tory Peterson, one of Teale's close friends, stopped here in 1953 with James Fisher on a memorable birding marathon along both coasts of North America, an expedition inspired in part by the success of *North with the Spring*. At the time the Lee Tidewater Cyprus Company owned the entire swamp, which was named the corkscrew for the crooked creek at its northern end. Rot-resistant bald cypress became a valuable commodity during World War II, for the wood was used to outfit the hulls of minesweepers and PT boats and as decking for aircraft carriers. Most of the big cypress had already been harvested and transported out of Florida by 1954 when the National Audubon Society, desperate to save a remnant of these magnificent old-growth trees, raised $170,000 to purchase the last remaining 3-mile stand. To access these 600-year-old giants, some of which rise 130 feet with girths of 25 feet, the Society constructed a 2-mile road augmented by a 2.25-mile circular boardwalk.

Corkscrew Sanctuary remains relatively undiscovered: in 2011 87,000 individuals paid the $10 entrance fee, most of which goes toward restoration. Florida Audubon spends $300,000 annually in an attempt to control invasive plants across the preserve. The list of targeted species for spraying includes Brazilian pepper, Balsam pear, cogongrass, Old World climbing fern, water lettuce, and earleaf acacia. When the sanctuary first opened, more than 6,000 pairs of wood storks nested in the crowns of the ancient cypress. However, since 2000 the number of nesting pairs has fluctuated between 1,700 and 10, and in the last three years not a single active nest has been recorded. Wood stork numbers have continually declined in the United States from a high of 30,000 in the 1930s to less than 5,000 nesting pairs today. Precise water levels dictate the success rate for nesting storks. The water must be deep enough during the wet season to provide an adequate fish spawn and yet shallow enough (15 to 18 inches) during the dry season to allow adult birds to stand and feed. Additionally, there must be sufficient water present around the base of the trees to prevent raccoons and other predators from reaching the eggs or just-hatched chicks. Ornithologists have determined that each wood stork chick requires 440 pounds of fish from hatch to independence in order to thrive. Unfortunately, this complex sequence of rainfall and drought now happens in South Florida once every six years.

Following the boardwalk, which passes over a pine upland that features an old plume hunters' camp, as well as a wet prairie and a marsh before reaching the cypress swamp, I pause to watch a rainbow-colored male painted bunting, several palm warblers and tree swallows, a red-bellied woodpecker, coots, a red-shouldered hawk, flocks of black vultures, white ibis, great-crested flycatchers, tricolored herons, and three pair of secretive black-crowned night herons. Then, as a light mist begins to descend in the late afternoon, I hear squeaking high up in the trees, where tattered fragments of abandoned stork nests remain. Four swallow-tailed kites, miraculous white birds out of some storm-tossed Coleridge poem, circle back and forth looking for a place to land. As the rain picks up, I take shelter with a group of teenagers who also appear interested in the birds above. They ask me if I have come to view the rare "Super Ghost" white orchid that blooms high up in these trees. Gradually, one by one we push out into the downpour and run along the boardwalk back to the education center.

During their second week in Florida, Edwin and Nellie accompanied Charles Broley, a retired Canadian banker who, at age sixty-seven, had "banded ten times as many eagles as any other living man." Broley concentrated his efforts along the state's west coast, where on average he located "an eagle's nest about every mile," according to Teale. Fifteen years later, Rachel Carson cited Broley's banding records to reinforce her argument that eagles were being poisoned by the indiscriminate use of pesticides. According to the author of *Silent Spring*, between 1952 and 1957, 80 percent of the nests Broley monitored failed to produce young, and in 1958 "Mr. Broley ranged over 100 miles of coast before finding and banding one eaglet." Declared an endangered species in 1967, eagles in Florida have made a dramatic comeback since Broley's passing. According to recent counts, there are now more than 1,100 pairs of nesting eagles in the state.

I planned to end my second week at Babcock Ranch in the company of Jim Wohlpart and Win Everham, faculty members at Florida Gulf Coast University. Another example of Florida's recent land acquisitions, Babcock, a public-private partnership, includes 73,000 acres adjacent to Fort Myers. According to Win, a contemplative, broad-shouldered disturbance ecologist about my age, this flat, dry ranchland "remains simply beautiful without regard to our long history of resource extraction from it." When complete, Babcock Ranch Preserve will feature the world's most environmentally friendly and sustainable city, according to its corporate promoters. Preliminary construction coincided with a downturn in the state's economy, and as a result, we pass by idle backhoes and look out across pink flagging where future ponds, bike paths, and boardwalks are envisioned.

Side by side we follow a sand road paralleling a ditch filled with wading birds. Herons anticipate our progress, lifting again and again from the bank, while egrets, like stationary kites, sail overhead. We listen to the plunk of bitterns, the rattle of kingfishers, and the scrape of alligators scrambling into the ditch. After an hour's walk, we stop to enjoy lunch and share our thoughts on the natural world.

"We need to pay more attention to how cultural cues place us in our environment," says Jim Wohlpart, an academic dean and extreme athlete. Turning to Heidegger, who wrote about "horizons of disclosure . . . the ways in which different cultures see the world revealing certain attributes and concealing others," Jim explains that our western, rigidly scientific view of nature is only one of several ways to understand human connections with the earth. In his classes he urges students to consider other "horizons"—other pathways by which we might reconceptualize our relationship with the land and thereby act differently.

"I tend to focus on natural cycles," Win responds, "events like hurricanes, fire, drought—and our role in their recovery. The truth is that this place around us is not what it was fifty years ago because of our actions. Frost, fires, hurricanes now impact it differently. I think we might actually have an obligation to keep our hands involved, a responsibility to manage the land, even if it means that we risk screwing things up."

Citing Aldo Leopold as his mentor, Win laments that too many people today bemoan change over time as inevitable loss. "They downplay our responsibility as the species that has had the most dramatic impact on the land for centuries, and at the same time they often fail to see the beauty. . . . Just look around us—the berm over there is built, so is the fence, and within 50 feet are four or five species introduced by humans—and yet this place is utterly beautiful."

We all agree that Babcock Ranch offers an ideal opportunity to test whether strategies of restoration can engage ordinary citizens in the creation of community, an idea put forth by William Jordan. Eighty percent of the land surrounding the five planned communities, where 18,000 houses are envisioned, is designated to remain a preserve, and more than half of the 17,000 acres of development will feature parks, greenways, and lakes. In *The Sunflower Forest* Jordan writes: "Ultimately, the future of a natural ecosystem depends not on protection from humans but on its relationship with the people who inhabit it or share the landscape with it." Convinced that passive preservation alone will not foster citizen engagement, Jordan proposes a four-stage "conversion process" designed to help individuals become active participants in Aldo Leopold's ideal land community. First, citizens must "achieve awareness of the other," a process that involves frustrations, facing limitations, and the experience of shame due to unforeseen miscalculations. As every homeowner knows, the process of reinhabiting a place involves mistakes as well as successes. Next, participants need to practice the "language of action and performance" by engaging in challenging physical labor that represents the economic basis behind any true ecological relationship. At Babcock, the topography of the land shaped the behavior of ranchers and farmers, and therefore some of their actions and habits are worth repeating. Third is the giving of gifts, an "open-ended exchange that transcends a purely economic relationship with the land." Finally, this cycle of gift exchange creates a "deepening sense of ambiguity," one that invokes a reliance on ritual and fosters a sense of community. "The act of restoration, precisely because it is inadequate and because it implicates the restorationist in the universal scandal of creation," according to Jordan, also "provides a context for achieving communion with creation."

The developers who oversee Babcock Ranch should make an effort to implement Bill Jordan's recommendations. For example, they might sponsor work days requiring strenuous physical labor supervised not by construction crews but by former ranchers and designed to build rapport among long-term inhabitants, new arrivals, and energetic schoolchildren. In addition, they might explore seasonal rituals and methods of gift exchange—activities like seed-saving and the removal of invasive species—to help residents acquire basic ecological knowledge and thereby dismantle structures of privilege that often interfere with community building. Given the size and scope of this project, undoubtedly many mistakes will be made, and some of these miscalculations will actually help residents come to better understand their home ground. It will be interesting to follow the progress of Babcock in the years ahead. All too often the vision that inspires partnerships like this one gradually fades as promoters seek to balance corporate profits with promises of ecological and community well-being.

More radical members of the conservation community have begun to envision another strategy—rewilding, a concept that moves beyond restoration and encourages the creation of corridors between protected parcels in order to facilitate the reintroduction of large predators like the wolf, the mountain lion, and the grizzly bear. They argue that the presence of these creatures, like the alligator I encountered in my kayak, will inspire residents and visitors to pay attention and interact with the landscape more intimately. According to wilderness advocates like Dave Foreman, Jack Turner, and J. B. MacKinnon, the presence of large predators may be necessary to rekindle our relationship with wildness: restoration alone will not engender the respect, mystery, and sense of awe that humans consistently lack today. Because Babcock's more than 70,000 acres allows unfettered access between sanctuaries north and south of Lake Okeechobee and the Charlotte Harbor Estuary on Florida's Gulf coast, it might serve as a model for introducing Florida panthers and perhaps even eastern wolves, and thereby assessing the reactions among human residents. It might lead to "the rewilding not only of a vanished species," according to MacKinnon, "but of something lost in ourselves."

Strategies focused on restoration or rewilding never crossed the mind of Edwin or Nellie Teale. Their plan to reawaken Americans to the natural world involved vivid depictions of places seldom seen. Rapid development was changing the character of these wild parcels even then, but the widespread use of pesticides, importation of exotic plants and animals, and battles between corporations and environmentalists lay years ahead. Adding to and protecting America's natural treasures seemed a sufficient challenge, especially given the fact that Alaska, with its vast stretches of wilderness, did not achieve statehood until 1959. When Teale considered the concept of restoration, it was his inner spirit he hoped to renew. As Peter Chidester observed, "*North with the Spring* is a Thoreauvian ramble in which the Teales focus their energies on the natural world in order to enact their own spiritual and intellectual rebirth."

On the long, dusty ride back from Babcock Ranch, I shared details from Teale's biography: his upbringing in Indiana, his devotion to Nellie, the loss of David, and how their odyssey following spring was designed to help them heal. Win Everham, seated behind me, listened quietly.

"Twenty days ago I lost my son, Daniel. He was just nineteen years old." Win offered nothing more, and the three of us rode the rest of the way in silence. As I prepared to leave, I tried to express how sorry I was for his loss and thanked Win for his time and insights. Two weeks later I received an e-mail from him reflecting on our time together.

His message began with some personal observations on spring's advance—"killdeers nesting, . . . and big flocks of tree swallows getting ready to head north." He apologized for "dumping" on me about his loss—"my grief is just this open wound that causes me to say whatever I feel." Finally, he tells me that as a result of our conversation, he's begun to take note of "what I see outside" in a journal he began in the wake of the tragedy. "It has helped me to see how much Teale wrote after his loss. It did not destroy him. He found meaning in the world around him and produced much that made a positive difference. And it seems to me he rediscovered joy in the world. Joy that I was scared might never be experienced again. Thank you so much for that gift!"

It is Teale who deserves this gratitude, for *North with the Spring* is his gift—a volume undertaken out of despair, written to placate grief, and offered to each of us—to those who have suffered agonizing personal loss, as well as those who have grown disheartened struggling in a diminished natural world.

Song of the Cardinal

When I came to the Creek, and knew the old farmhouse and grove at once as home, there was some
terror, such as one feels in the first recognition of a
human love, for the joining of person to place, as of
person to person, is a commitment to shared sorrow, even as to shared joy.

MARJORIE KINNAN RAWLINGS, *Cross Creek*

Ever "luscious and fruitful," according to Susan Orlean, with
its "newly minted land" and its "bright new sand," south Florida has sounded a Siren's call for nearly 100 years. The Teales
experienced Marco and Sanibel Islands just ahead of the real
estate boom that disfigured these offshore outposts. Teale
records fish shacks, sand roads, and ramshackle farms where
today high-rise office buildings and five-star hotels cast long
shadows across white sand beaches. A network of highways
now parallels the coast, and residential neighborhoods have
expanded their tentacles into every corner of the island. The
ten-car ferry that carried the couple to Sanibel has been replaced by a towering four-lane bridge. Once there, their "long
slow drive racked by washboards, chok[ed] in . . . clouds of shell
dust," has given way to bumper-to-bumper traffic from bridge
to beach. Even the view of the Gulf sky, once "burnished and

clear," is now eclipsed by mansions, some single-story post-modern structures stretched across the dunes, others garish pseudo-adobe monstrosities.

The Sanibel National Wildlife Refuge, established on the island two years before the Teales arrived, recorded rats and raccoons in the early years. Fewer than 40,000 tourists visited Sanibel in the early 1950s, and like Teale, most of them headed straight for the beach. By 1967, when the refuge was renamed to honor cartoonist and part-time resident J. N. "Ding" Darling, a causeway had been constructed across the inlet. According to the refuge's annual reports, this easy access changed everything. Real estate sales exploded; more than 218,000 tourists visited the sanctuary the next year, and "the solitude and wild beaches began to disappear."

Alligators and loggerhead turtles were plentiful on Sanibel Island before development limited their access. Refuge staff documented the first armadillo, opossum, and a visiting Florida panther during the 1960s, a decade in which a single pair of eagles on nearby Captiva Island repeatedly failed to produce a viable offspring. The Ding Darling Refuge instituted a wildlife drive to encourage tourism, ignoring conservationists like Edward Abbey, who called for the elimination of the automobile on all federal wildlife properties. In 1995 commercial buses and mopeds were prohibited along the 5-mile loop in favor of tram tours and single cars.

When I visit Ding Darling, the refuge is awash in chrome and heavy with exhaust fumes. Private automobiles are still welcome on the crushed gravel trails encircling the mud flats, and more than 500,000 visitors annually experience the sanctuary through their windshields. As a result I often stand alone with my binoculars, scanning the shoreline while engines hum and car doors slam to hurry viewers to the next spectacle. I yearn for a strategy adopted by the National Park Service at Shark Valley, another popular destination for bird watching I visited along the Tamiami Trail. Originally constructed by Humble

Oil, Exxon's predecessor, this 15-mile loop was given to the federal government in 1966 as oil exploration waned. Teale was an unlikely witness to the last phase of this process, for he noted drilling machinery in operation north of the Tamiami, as well as "a rusting mass of boilers . . . half-overgrown by weeds" to the south of the road.

I waited for thirty minutes behind dozens of cars for a space to open in the Shark Valley parking lot. An extended entrance road, a limited number of parking spaces, and a pleasant attendant are all components of the visitor strategy here. Once inside, I joined a community of walkers, bikers, and tram riders along a 5-mile stretch of shallow water. Herons, egrets, ibises, spoonbills, and a sizable number of alligators vied for our attention. Standing apart in space and yet connected in spirit, we watched a reddish egret perform its dizzy dance. Later, in the shade of the observation tower marking the halfway point, we traded stories while eating lunch. Nature, in the absence of automobiles, fosters a sense of community.

While most visitors retraced their steps, I elected to ride the less-traveled outer loop. Here shallow mudflats shimmered in the afternoon heat, and wading birds in small numbers clustered along shallow pools. Each drainage ditch beneath the bike path supported its own resident alligator, whose length seemed determined by the depth of available water. Gator hunting in the early decades of the twentieth century required stealth and superhuman patience. In their heyday, American tanneries processed 280,000 alligator hides valued at $420,000 each year. Almost a quarter of these hides originated in Florida.

Along "a great blinding white beach," Edwin and Nellie spent a February day shell hunting on Marco Island. While walking the tide line, they came upon "a large black sow" and later watched other pigs "roaming the beach like wild scavengers." Less than 500 people, most of them fisherman, made Marco Island their home in 1947. Today more than 17,000 residents compete for space along this 10-mile spit of land. The only pig to be found on Marco Island is the one stenciled on a barbeque sign.

I searched the dense grid of streets on Marco hunting not for shells but for what Teale had described as "the loneliest cemetery I have ever seen," set "a mile or more from the nearest shack." I eventually located this quaint burial ground, surrounded by office buildings in a residential neighborhood. Meandering up and down its rows, I finally discovered the stone Teale had called attention to. Nestled among towering live oaks, the marker reads: "William T. Collier, born in Tenn. March 12, 1815, died Marco Island, Florida October 30, 1902." William T. Collier, it turns out, was the first permanent European resident on this island, having sailed here with his wife and eight children in 1871. He bears no relation to real estate mogul Barron Collier, who subsequently purchased and later resold Marco Island. Near this headstone "worn by storms," Teale also noted a recent grave, "one so modern it represented a casualty in the war."

Edwin Way Teale loved cemeteries, the more remote the better. His record of graveyards on this trip included Bulls Island, Cape Cod, along the Hudson, and northern Vermont. Unlike other forms of architecture, burying grounds juxtapose civilizing forces and untamed nature. They suggest more than they inscribe—hinting at stories that connect inhabitants with the places where they once lived. Even small rural commemorative plots offer a portrait of the community at large. In addition, they tend to be left undisturbed, even when rapid development or preservation protocol obliterates all other evidence of human habitation. Teale's fondness for small, out-of-the-way graveyards satisfied multiple yearnings: they confer an air of serenity, they underscore one's own mortality, and they evoke the memory of absent loved ones. In addition, etched stones offer points of access, portals through which we can experience feelings of awe and transcendence. In border realms like these, "something sacred reveals itself" and "the land knows you are there."

The River Styx in northern Alachua County, a place "strange and eerie," "oppressive and yet enchanting," beckoned to Teale on his way to visit Marjorie Rawlings. Its black water, once covered in a "thick raft of hyacinths," flows no more. The skeleton of a decaying deer now marks the dry channel, and the "amphitheater of trees," once cloaked in Spanish moss, has been removed. A new bridge, a paved road, a scene of enchantment drained away. I continued on a few miles west to Micanopy, an important early settlement after the Florida Association of New York forged a 45-mile road through trackless wilderness in 1822. Organized around a circular common, the town's red-brick buildings and stately houses at first appeared little changed since 1900. However, every lawn was manicured, "Guests Welcome" hung from porches, and kitsch cluttered a former hardware store window. Only the bakery, where I purchased a loaf of fresh sourdough from an attractive young woman with Indian features, offered an air of authenticity.

A placard planted on the town common indicated that William Bartram, America's first-born naturalist, had visited this site in 1773 on his plant-collecting excursion. In his wanderings through Florida, Georgia, and the Carolinas, Bartram had sought out contact with the indigenous people. In Micanopy he encountered the Seminole chief who called himself the Cowkeeper, once a great warrior who had led his people against the Spanish. The Cowkeeper welcomed Bartram, prepared a feast in his honor, and granted him unfettered access to observe the ways of his tribe. Much of what we know about Florida's indigenous population and native flora we owe to William Bartram.

All travelers' journals, including those of Bartram and Teale, are filled with mishaps as well as scenes of enchantment. For instance, when my predecessor set out for Sanibel, he arrived too late for the ferry, followed the wrong road once there, and experienced a beach littered with decaying fish in a blazing hot sun. Unable to appreciate what he came to observe, Teale's "mind seemed dried out, hardened like putty left for years on a shelf." I too suffered a misadventure during my second week as I attempted to camp nearby Micanopy. My troubles began when the ranger at the entrance gate insisted that I pitch a tent. I paid the fee, rummaged through my gear, and set up the nylon shelter. Half an hour later, obviously doubting my word, the ranger blundered through my site. In response, I stuffed my pack with camping supplies, jumped on the bike, and peddled up and down sand roads looking for a remote campsite. When I passed a patch of desolate woods, something rushed from beneath the brush and collided with my bike pedals. Scrambling to avoid the contact, I ditched the bike and tumbled onto the ground. My assailant, a bizarre-looking creature, hissed at me from under a tangle of brush. I later learned that nine-banded armadillos are quite common in Florida today, although Teale makes no mention of these armored opossums. Armadillos migrated from Texas into Florida around 1900, and a second population, purported to have escaped from a traveling circus, began to multiply along the state's Atlantic coast. These ancient mammals are unusual in many ways, not the least of which is their method of reproduction, called polyembryony, meaning that a single fertilized egg gives rise to four identically sized and sexed offspring.

Ultimately, I settled on a sheltered spot beneath a clump of live oaks to spend the night. After stretching a tarp between trees and gathering sticks for a small fire, I listened to the sound of distant water and the rustle of nearby feet. A thin crescent moon offered little light, and I lay beneath the tarp alert to every sound. Sleep proved pointless, and in its place I imagined a herd of slowly encroaching feral hogs.

I broke camp at daylight, exhausted, stiff, and hungry. Peddling hard to vent my frustration, I snapped the bike chain in the soft wet sand. For miles I nursed my broken bike and finally collapsed when I reached my vacant tent. Before drifting off that morning I recalled a line from Teale: "I was glad at the thought that I would wake up in a new and different day."

⟋ ⟋ ⟋

Florida backroads still contain surprises—orange groves in which the same tree sports white blossoms, small green globes, and fully ripened fruit. Swallow-tailed kites glide over fields of clover festooned with hundreds of honeybee hives. And remnants of 1950s Florida can still be found. I walked the streets of Arcadia in De Soto County and discovered a coffee shop with Formica countertops and polished linoleum floor tiles. My waitress, dressed in pink, explained that the shouting I heard outside was a local resident who, for years, had harangued passersby with his street-corner sermons. On days when he wasn't preaching, the man worked the hardware counter at Walmart, where he hardly uttered a word. Frederic Remington visited this frontier town at the turn of the twentieth century in search of cowboy models for his western paintings. The original main street was rebuilt in brick following a devastating fire in 1905. Since then, Arcadians have mastered the art of adaptation, having suffered a cycle of boom and bust in phosphate mining, citrus, and the closing of two military airfields. Today it hosts the state's largest array of solar power.

Coastal Cedar Key, which I visited several days later, also appears to have escaped modernity. Front yards are littered with crab pots or garden tools, and residents welcome sightseers from wide front porches. The working waterfront on the edge of town has clearly contracted, and art studios are multiplying along the main boulevard. Nevertheless, inhabitants seem comfortable with themselves and with the pace of change in town. As my waitress at a local restaurant that looks out over the canal confided: "I'm a single mom and both of my boys know the sheriff by first name. How often does that happen in Florida?"

Cemetery on Atsena Otie Key in Cedar Keys National Wildlife Refuge.
Photo by author.

An historic marker along the beach at Cedar Key describes the town's early history. Eberhart Faber, an immigrant from Germany, arrived in New York looking for a source for splinter-free wood for pencil slats. Cedar Key's red cedar, a form of juniper, offered the perfect product, and Faber began to float whole logs from Atsena Otie Key to the mainland before shipping them on to Europe. In 1858 he constructed a slat mill on Atsena Otie and built a pencil factory in New York City. I kayak out to Atsena Otie, where the only evidence of this thriving industry is a cemetery, with unadorned graves dating from 1807 to 1916. A hurricane leveled the island town in 1896, and its 297 residents are now long gone. Since 1997 Atsena Otie has been part of the Cedar Keys National Wildlife Refuge, a thirteen-island preserve where more than 200,000 plume birds originally roosted and where more than 20,000 egrets, herons, pelicans, white ibis, and cormorants continue to nest today.

On Tuesday, March 11, six days after Edwin counted glossy ibis on Lake Okeechobee, he and Nellie arrived at Cross Creek, the home of celebrated writer Marjorie Kinnan Rawlings. Although the couple looked forward to this encounter, the two authors were temperamental opposites. Edwin, meticulous and reserved, appeared uncomfortable in the presence of the talkative, hard-drinking, chain-smoking celebrity. For her part, Rawlings greeted the couple warmly and seemed to intuit Edwin's fascination with his boyhood days. She suggested a drive out to the sandy plateau in the Ocala National Forest where, in a "secret and lovely place," according to Teale, where shafts of sunlight reflected "the pulsing flutter of sand grains," she rehearsed the story of Jody building his delicate fluttermill in her best-selling novel *The Yearling*.

Rawlings had prepared a picnic lunch of fried chicken, boiled eggs, potato salad, layer cake, and fresh oranges. Later that evening back at Cross Creek, she served them "boiled halves of grapefruit, scrapple, string beans, baking powder biscuits, mangoes, and a special food for the gods, the white heart of a cabbage palm." Even these culinary efforts proved insufficient, however, for although his published account lavishes praise, Teale's journal entry is less complimentary. "She is generous in the extreme, but not gracious or thoughtful. We had the feeling of being objects of charity."

As the chapter epigraph intimates, Rawlings formed a deep attachment to her Cross Creek home. She likely picked up on Edwin's melancholy frame of mind and his dissatisfaction with their Baldwin, New York, home. Central Long Island was rapidly becoming suburbia, so much so that Teale's treasured butterfly garden on a small vacant plot near their residence would soon disappear to make room for a new public school. Edwin recognized that it would take years before they could afford a rural retreat like Cross Creek. This blend of disappointment and envy perhaps explains Teale's failure to mention Rawlings' beautiful depiction of spring first published in 1942.

"Life now stirs and sap rises and the creatures mate and the snakes come out of their winter's lethargy," she had written. And while there is no single indicator of change in Cross Creek, "several spontaneous burstings" occur in February. Swamp maples show color, "cypresses' needles sprout," jessamine blooms yellow, and the redbud begins to flower. By the time Rawlings had written this evocative portrait, she had lived in this isolated community for more than a decade. Her love for its subtleties and complexities remain evident today.

I arrived at Cross Creek on the same March date as my predecessor. The redbud trees were already in bloom and the cypress branches had all leafed out. I walked first to the pier where Rawlings kept a rowboat docked and looked out across a river whose surface remains covered in water hyacinths. Introduced by a Japanese delegation visiting for the international cotton exposition in 1884, these attractive plants soon spread out of control, clogging up creeks and rivers across Louisiana and Florida. In *Cross Creek* Rawlings tells of her frustrations with water hyacinths while attempting to navigate the St. Johns River. Teale makes mention of this invasive species, recalling a letter he read in a Florida newspaper which suggested "that the hippopotamus be introduced to eat up water hyacinths." As ridiculous as this idea sounds today, a bill actually passed through Congress appropriating funds for the importation of African hippos. Those who spoke in support of this idea argued that hippopotami would not only eliminate choked waterways but they would also solve America's meat crisis. An article in the *New York Times* in 1910 heralded this proposal as "practical and timely," and it was only a series of administrative snafus that kept hippos from joining melaleuca trees, green iguanas, Burmese pythons, and water hyacinths in Florida.

Lifting the entrance gate to Rawlings' cracker home, now a state historic site, I notice a man feeding chickens in the side yard. Porches frame three sides of her white house—some are screened while others let in the morning sun. Massive oaks line the front drive, festooned with Spanish moss and sporting the same "tinge of green" and "infinitesimal rosy blossoms" Rawlings had observed. A smattering of orange trees, remnants of the original 74-acre grove she once tended, show white amid the cabbage palm, palmetto, and live oak forest across the street. As I settle back into one of the rocking chairs facing the road, I can smell breakfast cooking in an interior kitchen. A replica of Rawlings' bright yellow Oldsmobile remains parked in the makeshift garage. Her commitment to Cross Creek is everywhere evident: in the arrangement of flowerbeds, the positioning of fruit trees, the well-worn paths from garden to barn. She concludes her memoir with a passage focused on a "pair of red-birds" that, after nesting in an orange tree out back, bring their young to feed "in the crepe myrtle in the front yard." My stroll across her lawn takes in that crepe myrtle as well as the three-note staccato of a courting cardinal.

From the very beginning newcomers to Florida envisioned a paradise, "a fresh, free, unspoiled start." Many brought with them the frontier mentality Remington sought to depict, and this ethos of conquest as opposed to stewardship has defined the state's "snowbird" culture ever since. "Thousands of idle loungers pour down here every year," laments Ted Levin, "people without a home . . . whose only object seems to be to amuse themselves without the least consideration of future results." Little by little, this ethic has permeated many Florida communities. Individuals grow indifferent to their neighbors, special places are forgotten, and the town's authenticity, imbued with distinctive stories, gradually atrophies. Floridians have been crowing over progress for so long that a sizable proportion lack the courage to confront the visionless exploitation that continues to ravage their homeland.

Naturalist Robert Finch, writing about Cape Cod, recognized that a point exists beyond which individuals no longer care about a piece of land or an entire community. Once this line is crossed, what remains "is not some injured yet viable and salvageable entity" but "a collection of remnants no longer worth saving." Many Florida communities crossed this threshold in the decade following *North with the Spring*. For those that remain, some protected, many still vulnerable, their vitality rests with a handful of activists. Restoration literally means to bring back, to rediscover that part of our nature that we have neglected or suppressed. My early weeks in Florida, looking up at tattered stork nests, striding beside Paul Gray, exchanging stories with Anne Sullivan and Ken Huser, standing on Marjorie Rawlings' porch, have convinced me that restoration requires courage, humility, and constant commitment.

Drowned Circular Chasms

There was a great orifice, a drowned circular chasm
of greenish-white limestone dropping away for 185
feet. . . . This was Wakulla Springs, the largest and
deepest spring on the face of the earth . . . looking
straight down from a drifting boat, we seemed floating in a balloon over gorges and mountains.

EDWIN WAY TEALE, *North with the Spring*

In addition to the Everglades, Florida boasts a second set of
natural wonders: seventy-plus artesian springs concentrated
in the north-central portion of the state. When Teale visited
these remarkable upwellings, the water beneath him was
crystal clear, "pure, transparent . . . untainted by salt." Most
of these ebullitions are threatened today, defiled by the effects of adding 700 new residents every day for each of the
past fifty years. This sixfold population increase between 1950
and 2010, while mainly focused along the coast, has depleted
inland aquifers tapped to provide water for drinking, flush-
ing, washing cars, and greening golf course fairways. To make
matters worse, since 1990 the statewide average temperature
across Florida has been gradually creeping upward. In March
2012 it measured 70.2 degrees Fahrenheit, 4 degrees above normal, and 10 degrees above the Florida average in March 1947

as recorded by the Oceanic and Atmospheric Administration. Meanwhile, rainfall amounts needed to recharge these aquifers continue to decline. The March 2012 rainfall total across Florida averaged a meager 2.32 inches, as compared with 7.13 inches of rain in 1947, when a series of torrential storms battered the state's southern coast.

It seems difficult to imagine that 100 years ago residents and state officials complained about too much water. Today, although Florida leads the nation in water reuse, projections suggest that 24 million residents in 2025 will require 3.3 trillion gallons of water, a 34 percent increase. Depleting Florida aquifers has begun to make national news, as indicated by a *New York Times* article published while I traveled across the state. The flow rate at Silver Springs, Florida's best-known natural spring and its first commercial attraction, has dropped by one-third over the past decade. Even so, a wealthy Canadian rancher recently applied for a permit to extract an additional 13 million gallons from Silver Springs each day in order to support his organic grass-fed beef operation and service a planned slaughterhouse. According to Charles Lee of Florida Audubon, "Silver Springs' flow will stop in 12 years, by conservative accounting, and within 20 months if the worst models prove true." An ecosystem metabolism study of the adjoining Silver River concluded that Silver Springs is being impacted by excessive pumping of the Floridian aquifer system, polluted by inefficient use of fertilizers and ineffective wastewater management methods, and further altered by the invasion of nonnative plant and animal species. Collectively, "these stressors are changing the ecology and aesthetics of Silver Springs on a scale that was almost unimaginable as recently as 10 years ago."

Teale scheduled a visit to Silver Springs to meet Ross Allen, an internationally recognized herpetologist and wildlife figure who had gained notoriety by milking more than 150,000 poisonous snakes to supply antivenin for soldiers during World

Ross Allen entertains guests at his Silver Springs Reptile Institute. Photo by E. W. Teale. Edwin Way Teale Papers, Archives and Special Collections at the Thomas J. Dodd Research Center, University of Connecticut Libraries. Used with permission.

War II. He spent two days in Allen's company following and photographing the capture of diamondback rattlesnakes. He marveled at stories of serpents crawling loose along floorboards as the carefree adventurer drove around the state bagging dangerous reptiles. Equal parts promoter and scientist, Ross Allen paid collectors $1 per foot for poisonous snakes and offered a $100 prize for any specimen over 8 feet.

The strategy of posting bounties for the capture of big snakes has made a recent comeback in Florida. In 2013 more than a thousand individuals participated in the "python challenge," a promotional effort sponsored by the National Park Service aimed at reducing the number of these exotic undesirables. Taking a script from Ross Allen, Park staff offered cash prizes—$1,000 for the largest python, and $1,500 for the most snakes disposed of—during this monthlong challenge. A diverse group of outdoorsmen slogged through waist-deep water or skimmed across the surface in airboats, killing sixty-eight Burmese pythons. Having served its promotional purpose, the hunt was discontinued the following year.

Roadside nature provided a major tourist attraction in Florida before 1970, and the animals that escaped from these makeshift menageries represent some of the most troubling exotics today. As a naturalist, Teale was drawn to these amateur zoological parks, although he chastised himself for taking time to visit. At "Jungle Drive" along the lower Suwannee River, for instance, he expressed his frustration for contributing to the upkeep of an institution that featured a caged marsh hawk and a "wildcat that hissed, growled endlessly, and trembled all over with fear, . . . hatred and impotent despair."

Before the arrival of Walt Disney's Orlando empire in 1971, Silver Springs served as the state's most popular natural attraction, welcoming more than 800,000 visitors annually. Film footage from the period shows Ross Allen playing an important promotional role, wrestling alligators and pythons, handling rattlers and coral snakes, and milking venom to impress bystanders. The Springs' clear water appealed to the movie industry as well. The original Tarzan films and 100 episodes of Lloyd Bridges' TV series *Sea Hunt* were filmed on location here. Today, according to the brochure I picked up as I paid to park, Silver Springs Attraction promotes animal exhibits, glass-bottomed boat rides, zoo and botanical garden tours, and a shopping adventure at the Springside Mall—all for a single $39 entrance fee. I wish now I'd paid the price to see these attractions; however, I balked on a day that threatened rain. Instead, I learned from Assistant General Manager Terry Turner that nothing about Ross Allen or the legacy of his Reptile Institute remains. "When companies change hands, things have a way of vanishing." Turner encouraged me to visit the Silver Springs Historical Society, which operates out of the local elementary school and is open only on selected weekends.

The ecological and economic significance of these natural springs has prompted state lawmakers to purchase and protect twenty-one of them. I camped at several state parks, including Manatee Springs, whose clear water and "astonishing ebullition" had impressed William Bartram 200 years ago. At Manatee, Bartram reported seeing the "skeleton of a 'manate,' which an Indian had killed." West Indian manatees continue to migrate up the Suwannee River in winter to take advantage of the Springs' constant 72 degree freshwater. On several occasions, I watched four of these gentle, 1,000-pound sea cows glide in and out of the run connecting spring and river. Rising to the surface like Macy's Thanksgiving Day parade floats, with tiny whiskered faces, they glided through the water with a single stroke of their massive tails. The leader of the pod, the largest and palest, displayed deep scars across its back as it gently turned to nuzzle its partner. It's easy to imagine how sailors once mistook these lethargic giants for whales and how effortlessly they were able to slaughter the curious creatures for meat and oil. Teale included a "modern" tale of senseless butchery in his journal: "Five manatees swam into the bay at Sarasota and every one was killed by a man . . . who pumped lead into them, although it is a federal offense to kill one." Although the shooter was arrested and went to trial, in the end he was "released on the plea that what he had killed was not a manatee but . . . a sea monster!" Thus, according to Teale, Florida courts "make a mockery of conservation—and justice."

A second Suwannee River migrant, one apparently never observed by Teale, is the Gulf sturgeon, a strange plated anachronism that can reach 8 feet in length and can live up to sixty years. Female sturgeons head north from the Gulf of Mexico in January to locate spawning grounds often positioned just downstream from these natural springs. The males follow in

February or March, and both sexes return downriver between April and June. The largest population of Gulf sturgeon, estimated at 9,000 individuals, migrates back and forth in the Suwannee River. Listed as threatened in 1991, these bizarre-looking armored fossils are known to jump completely out of water, sometimes injuring boaters. I heard the splash of what I took to be a sturgeon as I paddled down the Suwannee one afternoon. These acrobatic leaps are believed to provide a primitive form of communication and group cohesion among the migrants.

In addition to natural springs, the state of Florida has purchased "type-specimen sanctuaries" to help protect and preserve other rare and endangered ecosystems. I waited for several days before securing a reservation at Paynes Prairie State sanctuary, a 16,000-acre limestone basin, with the Alachua Lake at its center. This giant sinkhole south of Gainesville forms the footprint of a dry prairie, where more than 270 species of birds have been identified. When Bartram visited this "vast plain of water in the middle of a pine forest," it contained "prodigious numbers of wild fowl, . . . cranes, herons, bitterns, plovers, coots," and "vast herds of cattle," pastured by members of the Seminole tribe.

From an observation platform park staff have erected along the south rim, I looked out across this vast treeless plain. Sandhill cranes danced in the foreground, wild horses galloped farther out, and a solitary bison, the last of the herd, grazed in the distance. Looking out on such a vista brought back memories of the Everglades' Anhinga Trail. On my way back to the campsite, I walked through a field littered with what I took to be foxholes, until at the entrance to one I caught a glimpse of a large, heavy-bodied gopher tortoise. These reptiles, now endangered, use their massive front feet to excavate burrows in the sandy soil. Teale described the "entrance to these 'gopher' holes" as dots of white sand along a patch of blackened earth where a fire had recently passed. Able to survive for more than half a century, gopher tortoises apparently evolved in partnership with increasingly rare dry habitants historically maintained by periodic wild fires.

⌐ ⌐ ⌐

Edwin elected to spend March 21, the first calendar day of spring, at Wakulla Springs, a resort destination south of Tallahassee. He and Nellie booked a room at the plush Edward Ball Lodge. This twenty-seven-room grand hotel, designed and constructed by Ball, a business partner of Alfred du Pont's, features marble floors, large canopied beds, and claw-footed bathtubs. The following morning, as the chapter epigraph records, the couple boarded a glass-bottomed boat where they marveled at the 185-foot limestone chasm where 250 million gallons of clear freshwater pulsed upward each day.

Arriving at Wakulla Springs State Park on March 21, I was disappointed to learn that the glass-bottomed boat rides have been discontinued. Increased nitrate levels from nearby wastewater treatment operations and agricultural runoff have stimulated the growth of algae and hydrilla, an aquatic invasive that threatens many Florida waterways. Not only has the water at Wakulla been rendered opaque, but the principal object that drew Teale there—the limpkins, odd, brown-speckled heron-sized birds—have also disappeared. The pontoon boat ride down the Wakulla River that Teale experienced remains operational, however, and I waited in line with a dozen other tourists for a seat on this same spacious riverboat. In place of limpkins, we spotted yellow-crowned night herons, beautiful thick-bodied waders with long black masks and spectacular imperial head plumes. Our guide indicated that several pairs of these birds now nest at the park each season. We also noted wood ducks, hooded mergansers, coots and purple gallinules, nesting osprey, belted kingfishers, and even, according to some passengers, a passing bald eagle. When I disembarked, dozens of swallowtail butterflies danced in and out of puddles beside

Edward Ball Lodge at Wakulla Springs State Park. Photo by author.

the spring. The chasm itself was crowded with children—youngsters splashing in the shallows, teenagers launching themselves from a diving platform, and infants in strollers mesmerized by this strange blue circle.

Limpkins, the sole remaining members of the family *Aramidae*, which are closely related to cranes and rails, vanished from Wakulla Springs in the 1990s. "One of the shyest of southern swamp birds" during Teale's day, they were already uncommon except in locations where conservationists like Edward Ball had offered them protection from hunters. As a result, the limpkins he and Nellie watched had "regained the fearlessness of their original dispositions." The pair spent the day wandering through a moist forest across from the lodge, where they heard limpkins cry and spotted them feeding on apple snails.

"That evening the dusk was filled with its 'kur-r-ee-OW!' or 'me-YOW!' rising to a caterwauling crescendo on the last syllable."

I was looking forward to an evening filled with these sounds. As limpkin numbers at Wakulla State Park began to decline, ecologists first theorized that the turbid water and excess nitrates might be responsible. However, neither hypothesis seemed to explain their sudden departure. Dana Bryan, environmental policy coordinator for the Florida Park Service, suggested that weather was the more likely culprit. Limpkins feed almost exclusively on half-dollar-sized apple snails, which lay their eggs just above the water line on various aquatic plants. The year 1993 was relatively dry, and so the eggs hatched normally. The next year, however, was remarkably wet: water levels were 2.5 times normal in June, 4 times normal in July, and 2.5 times normal in August. Bryan speculates that apple snail eggs drowned, and the birds that year were forced to seek food elsewhere. Their failure to return in any of the following years has made ecologists like Bryan uncomfortable, especially given how difficult it will be to predict what "normal rainfall" might mean in the years ahead. One glimmer of hope for limpkins appears to be the accidental introduction of exotic island apple snails, a more robust cousin that arrived in Florida several decades ago. To the surprise of the environmental community, limpkins and Everglades snail kites, another federally protected species that feeds on these snails, have readily adapted to the larger food source, and as a result they have begun to increase their numbers and extend their breeding range.

No record of Edwin Way Teale at Wakulla Springs remains—hotel ledgers were unavailable, and no one I asked remembered his name. He might well have appreciated this anonymity, for he left the lodge in a state of withdrawal: "Nothing depresses me more," he wrote, "or makes me draw into my shell more than such surroundings. I am a shy, timid, scared, incorrigible mouse!" After spending time with these journal entries, I could imagine Nellie, seated beside him, soothing her husband's tarnished ego.

I elected not to spend the night at Wakulla and headed north into Georgia late that afternoon. I'd managed to avoid the Florida I had dreaded—countless shopping malls, interstate traffic jams, arrogant tourists, and crowded beaches. Instead, I had witnessed and experienced spectacular natural settings. With a few notable exceptions like the limpkins, the features of spring that my predecessor had documented are still available after sixty-five years. Of the 119 bird species he observed in Florida, all are with us today. Projections for the years ahead are not so positive, however. A recent report by the Audubon Society forecasts that climate change will disrupt half of North America's bird species and, more ominously, that almost one-quarter of these will lose "more than half of their current climatic range by 2050 without the potential to make up losses by moving to other areas."

Edwin Teale could not imagine Wakulla Springs without the cry of limpkins. "It was the voice of the dark, the swamp, the vast wilderness of ancient times. It links us—as it will link men and women of an even more urbanized, regimented, crowded tomorrow—with days of a lost wildness." The link he imagined seems in the process of being broken. His portrait of old Florida—its ramshackle fishing shanties, laundry strewn across barbed wire fences, one-room cabins on dead-end dirt roads—has disappeared. Remnants of the ecosystems he recorded have been protected and preserved in locations like Paynes Prairie, Shark Valley, and Babcock Ranch. As I drive north along the Suwannee River, I recall sites unavailable to Teale: Hells Bay, Bradley Key, Corkscrew Swamp, and the Wildlife Refuge at Cedar Key, where some 20,000 long-legged waders return each spring to build their nests. Creatures, strange and now familiar, come to mind: anhingas and armadillos, burrowing owls and bison, crocodiles and "crying birds," gopher tortoises and glossy ibis, reddish egrets and roseate spoonbills, swallow tailed kites and West Indian manatees. These along with the promise that 9.3 million acres of Florida wild lands will remain forever undeveloped and available to the public. A line from Tennyson's poem "Ulysses"—"Tho' much is taken, much abides"—carries me forward.

Land of Trembling Earth

Henry Bennett went down there to go in swimming—him and his brother. . . . And one of 'em
jumped off ahead of the other. . . . And directly he
seed his brother's foot come up. . . . He knew there
was something the matter with him. And he drug
'em, 'gator an' all, out to dry land. The 'gator had the
boy by the head, but turned him loose when they got
out to the land. . . . And I see the boy many a time
with the scars on both sides of his head. An' there
weren't no hair on the scars.

OWEN THRIFT, *Okefinokee Album*

Some 500 miles north of the Everglades lies the Okefenokee
Swamp, another vast, trackless wetland, composed not of limestone but of peat. This "Land of Trembling Earth," as the Native
people knew it, seems older and more mysterious, obscured
by what Teale called "curtains behind curtains." He and Nellie
had planned to spend three days exploring the swamp from
Lem Griffis' fishing camp located on the remote southern side.
However, heavy spring rains forced them to change their plans.
According to the Fish and Wildlife Refuge Narrative Report,
water levels in the Okefenokee during the first four months
of 1947 rose six inches above normal. In disappointment, the
pair turned north to Waycross and followed the Vereen Bell

Memorial Highway to the Okefenokee Swamp Park, a privately operated tourist attraction located on Cowhouse Island that had opened only a year before. "This is the most interesting park I know—worth a dozen Silver Springs," Teale noted soon after they arrived. He climbed a 60-foot wooden observation tower, where he saw carpenter bees, a great blue heron, two large black-shelled turtles, a red-shouldered hawk, a water turkey, and several species of warblers. The photograph he took from this height shows a network of shallow boat runs, each bathed in sunlight between spindly cypress and thin-branched pines.

Today the southern entrance to the Okefenokee Wildlife Refuge features a paved road meandering 17 miles north of Fargo to its terminus at Stephen Foster State Park, established in 1967. I travel beside the scorched path of the Honey Prairie Fire, the largest conflagration to strike the swamp in the past seventy-five years. Almost 500 square miles of forest burned for almost a year as a result of low water, high winds, and available fuel, much of which included dead and diseased pines. Fire is a regular feature of the Okefenokee ecosystem; however, the extent of this blaze, which closed the refuge for months, worries officials as a harbinger of things to come. Prolonged periods of drought, coupled with more severe storms and greater tree mortality due to invasive insects, are predicted across the Southeast in the years ahead.

Only two dozen campers have claimed sites within the park, and I spend a pleasant hour walking the Trembling Earth Nature Trail, with its boardwalk out into a peat bog, and visiting the nearby education center with exhibits on turpentine production and early homesteading. Mosquitoes force me into the truck early that evening, where I listen as barred owls call to one another through the pines. The next morning I paddle out to Billy's Island, the second largest of the sixty islands in the Okefenokee Refuge. At one time a railroad penetrated the 35-mile stretch of swamp to reach this island, where a logging

Cypress trees in the Okefenokee Swamp in 1947. Photo by E. W. Teale. Edwin Way Teale Papers, Archives and Special Collections at the Thomas J. Dodd Research Center, University of Connecticut Libraries. Used with permission.

camp once stood, complete with theater, machine shop, doctor's office, and commissary along with forty-nine houses. Between 1901 and 1927 some 2,000 loggers cut and processed more than 425 million board feet of cypress, red bay, and pine, which represented between 40 and 60 percent of the timber in the entire swamp. Among the casualties of this logging incursion was a mature sweet gum forest on Minnie's Island where ivory-billed woodpeckers made their home. The last of this species to be seen in the Okefenokee was a single bird shot and killed in 1912.

The canoe trails that access the Okefenokee's opaque water, the color and texture of boiled coffee, meander around massive bell-shaped bald cypress trunks whose distant canopies and gossamer leaves shroud the sun. Many of these routes, originally kept open by alligators, were first explored by Seminole people long before white swampers arrived. Today Billy's Island supports a maturing forest, in which massive iron cylinders, debris left behind by the Hebard Lumber Company, lie rusting. A small fenced-in cemetery includes several graves of the Lee family, the first white settlers to arrive on the island. Three generations of Lees cleared and cultivated 50 acres of land in the middle of Billy's Island. The family lived together in a single house before the lumber company pushed them out. On my slow-paced walk around the island, I find evidence of turkey, deer, fox, and perhaps even a bobcat, a relatively common species in the refuge.

Later that day, I paddle out to Minnie's Lake, another location Teale had hoped to visit. As the sun recedes along this route, those "curtains behind curtains" grow darker. I encounter a group of volunteers at work replacing portions of a shelter damaged in the fire. Among them is an older man who introduces himself as Tom. Like the others, he's grown up close to the swamp, and he shares stories of hunting bears using dogs and spending one summer hauling 90-pound buckets of gooey turpentine sap through the Georgia woods in 100 degree heat.

Cypress trees in the Okefenokee in 2012. Photo by author.

It's evident that he and his co-workers love these borderlands, and Tom recalls how his father—like many local men—once hunted, fished, and guided outsiders through the maze of boat trails in all seasons of the year.

As early as 1931, a proposal was put forward for the federal government to purchase the Okefenokee and establish a wildlife sanctuary. A special committee on conservation that visited the swamp that year concluded that it would make an attractive and valuable sanctuary for indigenous species. In 1937, President Franklin D. Roosevelt declared 396,000 acres of this swampland a national wildlife refuge. A decade later, Teale applauded the courage behind this conservation effort: "In a country where 100,000,000 acres of marshes already have been drained, this greatest swamp of the eastern seaboard promises to retain permanently the fascination of the untamed." Since 1947, these acres have grown considerably wilder: large populations of alligators, bears, and sandhill cranes have reappeared; armadillos have joined raccoons as a common sight; and in 1968 refuge officials spotted the "first beaver since the refuge was established." In an effort to discourage development of any kind, Congress designated most of these 400,000 acres a wilderness preserve in 1973.

The prohibition of all forms of hunting in the swamp after the federal government gained possession forced the exodus of many local swampers. Although similar restrictions had caused little controversy when applied to smaller acquisitions like Pelican or Bulls Island, inhabitants living on farms adjoining the Okefenokee could no longer kill the bears, bobcats, and alligators that threatened their livestock. As a result, most sold their holdings to timber companies, and those who remained took jobs as employees for the newly established refuge.

Teale hired one of these local swampers, a man named Will Cox who was "big and raw-boned, square-headed, with one gold front tooth." Cox poled the couple around in his flat-bottomed boat and regaled them with tales about his encounters and adventures. On this trip Nellie saw her first live wild alligators—sometimes "only its eyes, like bumps on a floating log," and at other times its entire length basking on a low hummock. Alligator hides once fetched as much as $3.75 per foot on the black market, and herpetologist Ross Allen, who kept records in Florida between 1929 and 1947, compiled a staggering total of 1,769,000 skins. As supplies dwindled in Allen's home state, poachers ventured north into the Okefenokee in search of quick profits. Refuge reports throughout the 1950s indicate that officers spent most of their time patrolling the waterways in search of trespassers. In 1956, for example, during one month more than 100 alligators were illegally stripped of their hides and left in the swamp to rot.

Such intense pressure on these reptiles apparently changed their nesting behaviors. According to a government study conducted in the Okefenokee in 1975, only 8 percent of nested alligator eggs hatched. The researchers noted that lack of aggressiveness by the female appeared to be responsible for these high levels of egg predation. They theorized that as a result of decades of poaching, female alligators had grown timid. Thus when opportunistic black bears caught sight of a nest, the mother alligator, conditioned to hide from danger, refused to defend her eggs. Alligators have gradually overcome their timidity, and today more than 10,000 thrive in the Okefenokee Swamp beside large numbers of bears and bobcats. By the time I encountered Tom and listened to his stories, I had paddled close to several dozen lounging gators, sunning themselves along either bank. The successful interactions among bears, alligators, and thousands of tourists who access the swamp via kayak and canoe has encouraged the proponents of rewilding, who argue that humans must reconnect and live in harmony with a wilder, more dangerous world.

As the chapter epigraph suggests, alligators figure in many Okefenokee stories. Francis Harper, a young Cornell naturalist assigned to conduct research in the swamp as early as 1912, collected and preserved many of these tales. With his wife, Jean Sherwood, he later built a house and settled on Chesser Island. Jean was largely responsible for alerting President Roosevelt to the natural beauty of the swamp, for she had tutored Roosevelt's children before marrying Harper. After they settled, she wrote letter after letter imploring the president to withhold funds for a proposed canal project in the swamp, and she described the remarkable plethora of creatures that inhabited the Okefenokee. When her husband published the *Okefinokee Album*, he included many reminiscences by men and women who had grown up fishing, trapping, and hunting black bears before the refuge was established. In one anecdote, Hamp

Mizell describes a day in which his brother and two other men shot and killed a large bear. "They hauled him into the boat an' rounded him up against a seat, lying there this-away, till he got stiff. The next morning when they come home, they put the 'gators they had killed in the end of the ditch my father had dug out in the prairie, so the sun wouldn't shine on 'em and spoil 'em."

Later that day, as Hamp walked out to help skin the bear, his favorite dog bolted ahead of him. "Thinking the 'gators, with their bulk sticking out, were just some logs," the dog trotted out on top of them. "'Bout that time he noticed they were alligators, and jumped into the boat. And there he run into the bear kind of sittin' up. An' he lit out of there with all four legs stuck out sideways—like a flying squirrel—and him a-hollerin' for all he was worth."

On the paddle back from Minnie's Lake, I spotted a red-cockaded woodpecker high up in a pine and observed my first prothonotary warbler, one of Teale's favorite birds, a beautiful bold little creature with bluish wings and a lustrous golden throat. It darted across the channel, flitted from branch to branch, and finally scolded me from the opposite bank. I also glimpsed another bird Teale identified with the swamp, the American bittern, a secretive creature known to locals as the "sun gazer" due to its habit of squatting motionless with its head stretched skyward to avoid detection. A couple from Connecticut invited me to dinner that evening: like so many others I would encounter, they knew and admired the seasonal writings of Edwin Way Teale.

In my conversation with Tom, he suggested that I might want to visit the eastern side of the Okefenokee, where open "prairies" take the place of cypress stands. Beginning in 1891, the Suwannee Canal Company repeatedly attempted to drain this portion of the swamp. Over the next decade, Captain Henry

Jackson spearheaded an effort to construct a 13-mile ditch designed to remove surface water so the underlying peat could be plowed and planted in rice, sugar cane, and cotton. The plan, which began by ditching at the rate of 44 feet per day, ultimately failed when work crews were unable to keep the canal walls from collapsing.

I paddle out along a remnant of "Jackson's folly" for several miles, waving back at gawking tourists seated in canopied pontoon boats. When I veer off to explore the shallow byways leading to Chesser and Grand Prairies, the open sky and shallow water bring back images of Nine Mile Pond in the Everglades. In place of periphyton, the surface here is covered in spadderdock lilies, floating bladderwort, and beautiful golden club, called "Neverwet" by locals. Gingerly, I paddle around another dozen alligators, several of them more than 12 feet long, sprawled across grassy hummocks. In the distance, herons and egrets, as well as an energetic osprey, glide back and forth in search of food. That afternoon, clouds move in and a steady drizzle falls as I retrace my route back across the prairies.

The next morning, I bike to the historic Chesser family homestead located on a small island south of the visitor center near Folkston. Restored to its original condition, the house, built of yellow pine, features an inviting front porch reminiscent of Marjorie Rawlings' cracker home. In addition to four bedrooms, an indoor kitchen, and an outdoor bathroom, outbuildings include a smokehouse, chicken coop, syrup shed, corncrib, and hog pen. According to the brochure, the Chesser family remained in this residence until the 1950s, hoping for a change in government policy. It was not until 1962, however, that Congress passed the Refuge Recreation Act, reversing earlier restrictions and sanctioning activities like hunting as well as broader access to sensitive areas so long as it did not interfere with the primary purpose of wildlife preservation. The Okefenokee Refuge responded by sponsoring its first deer hunt in 1980.

On my ride back to park headquarters, I nearly collide with a roadside alligator, and then screech to a halt to avoid running over a pygmy rattlesnake making its way across the asphalt. Watching this creature coil in angry response, I recall Teale's photo in *North with the Spring* where, with steady hands, he lifts a 4-foot, thick-bodied diamondback using only a flimsy snake hook. I remember my own youthful fascination with reptiles of every kind. As often as I could extract myself from summer chores, I would strike out for granite ledges on a hilltop behind my uncle's farmhouse in Pennsylvania. Carrying a long, forked stick, I crept along the backside of these outcroppings, peering into crevices for sunning blacksnakes. They often lay loosely coiled in the late afternoon, and when I spotted one, I inched forward on hands and knees. The rush of excitement as the snake whipped wildly beneath my stick and the feel of its cool, shiny-scaled "neck" and powerful pulsing torso wrapped around my arm remain with me to this day. I usually tossed my captive into a hogshead barrel I kept in the yard and helped to free it the next morning if it hadn't already escaped.

I never manage to visit the private Swamp Park where Edwin and Nellie stayed, although I follow the same back roads they traveled on my way moving north. Southern Georgia once supported a vast forest of longleaf pine, but these magnificent trees were gone by the turn of the twentieth century. In their place Teale spotted "chopped or sawed [pine logs] of six or seven feet for trucking to the slash-pine paper mills." According to Janisse Ray, a Georgia native whose Red Earth Farm in Reidsville forms my next stop, "Nothing is more beautiful, nothing more mysterious, nothing more breathtaking, nothing more surreal" than a longleaf forest. Thousands of longleaf seedlings are now planted at dozens of southern wildlife refuges each year, and M. C. Davis, an entrepreneur turned conservationist, has invested in 8 million longleaf seedlings planted on his 51,000-acre corridor between Elgin Air Force Base and the Apalachicola National Forest in Florida's Panhandle. If his efforts are successful, individuals born in the twenty-first century may once again experience the breathtaking mystery of a longleaf pine forest.

Along my route to Reidsville I pass container trucks spewing scraps of garbage on their way to massive rural landfills. These mountains of trash recall the "disagreeable, penetrating odors" Teale attributed to the region's paper mills. Work crews, composed of young African American men in orange jumpsuits watched closely by shotgun-toting correctional officers, most of whom are white, represent the most recent chapter in southern segregation. Overt racial discrimination bothered Edwin and Nellie throughout their southern travels. Not only were they required to eat and sleep in "Whites Only" establishments but Edwin lamented that "poorer filling stations have no accommodations for Negroes." He described at length one scene in which the "continual ever-present sense of injustice and unfairness" galled him. On a Florida highway a patrolman stopped to issue a warning to two men—one white and one black—fishing off the same bridge. "The policeman walked past the white man without molesting him and began to bellow at the negro . . . this two-standard code in everything must drive the intelligent and the sensitive negro to despair." Unfortunately, the author of *North with the Spring* lacked the courage to publish such remarks.

Janisse Ray, the author of six books on Georgia natural history, purchased her Reidsville home with her husband, Raven Waters, in order to develop an environmental education center and model for sustainable living. On 46 acres, the couple raises sheep, pigs, goats, turkeys, ducks, guineas, rabbits, and chickens for meat. They milk a few cows and rely on a 1-acre garden to supply them with fresh fruits and vegetables. They also have become passionate about beekeeping, cheese-making, brewing, heirloom seed-saving, and trading or selling produce at local farmers markets as far away as Savannah. Ambivalent about the current value of writing, Janisse regrets that "words no longer have the same power to inspire change in young people as they once did in me." Instead, she has begun to place her hopes in the growth of small, diversified farms, many initiated by young women, and in the younger generation's enthusiasm for locally grown organic food.

Watching Janisse and Raven stretch and mold mozzarella at the kitchen sink that evening, I sense the deep satisfaction they take in productive farmwork. Outside, Raven shows me his bee yard, where we chat about colony collapse disorder and its likely causes. Beekeepers in France and Germany have petitioned their governments to place a ban on the systemic pesticides they believe responsible for altering honeybee behavior. I search for words to describe the emptiness I experienced after losing a strong colony of bees. That same feeling, multiplied ten times, sweeps over me as Raven moves into the garden. My father spent countless hours weeding, hoeing corn, and filling bushel baskets with ripe tomatoes. His obsession to grow far more than the family could consume, I suddenly understand, was motivated not by early hunger, as I had assumed, but by fond memories of working side by side with his own father.

The next morning I set out for Charleston, South Carolina, where Teale spent two days and where I plan to spend the weekend with our oldest daughter, Meade, and her husband, Henry Goodwin. Along the way I pass a scene straight out of Teale's journal: "tin shacks and wooden racks" that display a variety of woven, sweetgrass baskets. African American women in brightly colored dresses gather in clusters beside their wares. Unlike my predecessor, I stop to chat, learning that only a few of these baskets are still made by hand, following a pattern passed down through generations. Later, in the center of the city, the three of us tour Charleston's narrow streets via a horse-drawn carriage and visit the natural history museum that Teale found noteworthy.

We saunter past the home of Herbert Ravenel Sass, a fellow nature writer Teale visited on his excursion. The older

Sass lamented that wild turkeys remained too little protected and that he could "never recall such a peculiar and backward spring." In the large egret and heron rookeries he was familiar with, Sass found "no nesting activities" and cypress trees with "no green on them." Spring in downtown Charleston this year is well advanced: dogwoods and azaleas have burst into bloom, and the smell of wisteria wafts down cobblestone streets. Nationally, the temperature in March has averaged 51 degrees, which is 8.6 degrees above the norm. The readings in South Carolina are almost 10 degrees above their annual average.

With its narrow streets and side-facing edifices, Charleston reminds us of northern cities like Portsmouth, New Hampshire, or the waterfront neighborhoods of Quebec. Bill Bryson once called Charleston the "most becoming American city he had ever seen," citing parallels with Naples, Italy. Teale, however, complained of clogged intersections, one-way streets, dilapidated tourist cabins, and unsightly oil spills marring the waterfront. According to our carriage guide, the city's charm stems from neglect, for no one had the money to tear down and refurbish its abandoned edifices. As a result, much of the original architecture remained intact when the fervor for civic improvement swept across the south. Thus while places like the Okefenokee (where Herbert Sass reported "hardly one alligator") have grown progressively wilder, many southern cities like Charleston have undergone renewal and refinement. Along the same boardwalk where Nellie counted half a dozen black skimmers, we pass flower vendors and warehouses in front of which shackled African slaves once stood. Looking out toward Fort Sumter, the sea is calm today, and the dire predictions regarding its future appear far off. According to climatologists, Charlestown remains one of the most vulnerable metropolitan areas along the entire East Coast.

. . . **7**

A Splendid, Unforgettable Week

There is a certain exciting moment of transition
when the powers of darkness begin to conquer and
our flaming campfire, lonely on a lonely beach, in
the immensity of the enveloping gloom, seems a
kind of symbol of courage and faith and hope. Here
is safety, warmth, protection. Here is a little tent or
igloo of light, a shelter against the awesome and the
unknown.

Edwin Way Teale, Journal of *North with the Spring*

Of all the wild sanctuaries Edwin and Nellie visited in their
pursuit of spring, Bulls Island was their unquestionable favorite. Here conditions were perfect—a week of sunshine after
near constant showers, freedom from their automobile, privacy from other sightseers, and thousands of newly arrived,
migrating birds. As the opening epigraph hints, Edwin was
able to suppress those "guilty feelings for all that David cannot enjoy" by immersing himself in long leisurely sojourns in a
place that proved to be a "Mecca for naturalists."

Located just 3 miles off the South Carolina coast and 20
miles north of Charlestown, Bulls Island was at the time already part of the Cape Romain National Wildlife Refuge. Today the complex of islands contains the most intact maritime

forest along the Eastern Seaboard. Like many other barrier islands, Bulls had been purchased in the 1920s by a single individual and used as a hunting camp and weekend retreat. Gayer Dominick, a New Yorker by birth, built a house for his family and guests after he and several of his investment partners developed a passion for duck hunting. After purchasing the island, Dominick dredged Moccasin Pond, the only expanse of freshwater, and installed dikes and impoundments to create four new ponds—Upper and Lower Summerhouse, House, and Big Pond. Although he continued to expand the network of sand roads around the island, his fondness for Bulls quickly began to wane. In 1936 he donated the entire island to the U.S. Fish and Wildlife Service, leaving behind all of his personal belongings, which included an account book of the island's history that Teale read and copied.

The couple boarded a ferry on April 7 at the invitation of refuge manager Joe Moffitt and his wife, Margaret. Similar in age and temperament, these unassuming hosts became "two of the most congenial people we met on the trip." In their company, Edwin and Nellie spent "a splendid, unforgettable week" sauntering sand roads, observing wild creatures, and listening to the ebb and flow of the sea. Alone on this remarkable refuge, Edwin filled fifty-five journal pages, three times his weekly average, and took hundreds of photographs documenting their stay. Here, in joyous solitude, "courage and faith and hope" began to grow.

Like most wildlife refuges, Bulls Island has remained relatively undisturbed. Visitor services coordinator Tricia Lynch invites me to spend three nights in the Dominick house. She also arranges for David McLean, an accomplished local birder, to join us on this excursion. On April 4 I meet my host at the Garris Landing dock, and we follow Teale's path out to the island. In little more than an hour, I am standing at the same kitchen table where Edwin and Nellie once ate, conversed, and made plans.

View from Bulls Island's lookout tower. Photo by E. W. Teale. Edwin Way Teale Papers, Archives and Special Collections at the Thomas J. Dodd Research Center, University of Connecticut Libraries. Used with permission.

After unpacking the boat, I make my way up a 125-foot metal observation tower located beside the Dominick house. Like my predecessor, I can feel the sway of the iron staircase in the wind. At the top a glass-enclosed lookout hut, thick with dust and littered with "little heaps and windrows of dried wasps," offers shelter. From this vantage high above tree line, I note the gap in the forest to the northeast that marks the site of an early eighteenth-century fort beside Jack's Creek. The theory is that this circular structure erected from fragile tabby, a mixture of shells and limestone, served as a lookout station for pirate ships, prevalent in the waters around nearby Charlestown harbor.

View from the same tower in 2012. Photo by author.

Out beyond the island in this direction stretches mile after mile of maritime wetlands, mostly spartina and salt grasses, with the same "silvery snakes of inlet rivers" zigzagging through them. To the east as far as I can see lies the ocean, and closer in I recognize Boneyard Beach by its frowzy tangle of bleached and weathered oaks, palmettos, and cedars littering the shore. The rise and fall of the surf along this deserted strand offered a welcome respite to the road-weary couple. Beyond the waves, seabirds like the northern gannet and storm petrel that seldom make contact with land feed in the choppy spray.

Turning south, I glimpse a narrow channel beyond which lies Capers Island, Bulls' smaller cousin, occupied by at least four dwellings visible from this distance. The calmer waters along Bulls' southern tip beckon summer boaters, who picnic on the beach and avoid the estuary where snowy egrets have located a rookery. At Tricia's invitation, I later photograph six females, with elaborate breeding plumage and delicate golden feet, as they rise from their nests exposing bluish-white eggs. Before descending, I work my gaze full circle, returning to the refurbished boat dock and retracing our channel homeward.

Many of Teale's photographs of Bulls Island feature a dark canopy of trees with cathedral-like shadows cast across the sand. These views are uncommon today, for in 1989 Hurricane Hugo made a direct hit, snapping 95 percent of the tall pines and wreaking havoc with the uppermost branches of the massive live oaks, once "fern-bearing and hoary." As a consequence, the trails I explore offer sunlit vistas with a tangle of understory shrubs. According to a Fish and Wildlife annual report for the year in which Hugo struck, 150 mph winds generated 19-foot waves that virtually inundated the island. Half of the deer population drowned, and one-third of the 30 turkeys, which numbered over 100 when Teale visited, were washed out to sea. Fewer than a dozen wild turkeys, none of which I detect, remain on the island.

Teale found it odd that neither foxes nor marsh rabbits had made their way out to Bulls Island. In the decades after his visit, Fish and Wildlife staff introduced a much more controversial predator, the endangered red wolf. The first pair of wolves relocated here swam back to the mainland, disquieting residents of McClellanville and threatening the success of the program. However, the government persisted, and over the next two decades twenty-six red wolf pups were reared on the island. The project was discontinued in 2004 due to declining revenues and the high mortality rates among adult red wolves released in locations across the Great Smoky Mountains National Park. According to Tricia Lynch, momentum is building to reestablish the breeding program on Cape Romain. Without question, wolves would change the ecology of Bulls, perhaps in unpredictable ways. After all, almost no one predicted that re-leasing gray wolves in Yellowstone National Park would trans-form the diversity of species along stream corridors.

Cape Romain continues to serve as a repository for other en-dangered animals, especially loggerhead sea turtles. Beginning in mid-May, female loggerheads, which can weigh up to 450 pounds, haul themselves out onto these barrier island beaches to lay their eggs. When Teale visited, no one knew for certain how many turtles nested on Bulls or how many eggs were laid on its shores. William Baldwin, a young biologist who answered many of these questions, met Teale on Bulls and demonstrated his turtle-tagging methods. Baldwin was the first biologist to document that the same turtle visits a beach multiple times in order to lay successive clutches of eggs. He also recorded as many as "600 loggerhead egg nests in one season on Cape Romain beaches" during his ten-year study. When these num-bers began to plummet in the 1970s, refuge staff constructed predator proof hatcheries, transplanted turtle eggs, monitored temperature and rainfall data, and released young turtles back into the ocean. As a result of these efforts, where volunteers now contribute 5,000 hours each spring to protect nests and preserve hatchlings, Cape Romain managed 1,676 loggerhead nests in 2012, a new record.

Along its beaches, its mudflats, and its freshwater ponds, Edwin and Nellie delighted in identifying some seventy spe-cies of birds. Their list included black-bellied plovers, spotted sandpipers, willets, ruddy turnstones, and "the big sight of the day—seven oystercatchers with their great lacquered red bills and their brilliant wing pattern in flight." Oystercatchers were uncommon at the time, and monitoring these birds has remained a high priority. South Carolina today is home to over a third of an estimated 10,000 oystercatchers that winter on the Atlantic and Gulf coasts. Studies indicate that 50 to 60 per-cent of these birds select Cape Romain. Following a 20 percent decline on the refuge between 1988 and 2004, conservationists stepped up efforts at predator control, mudflat protection, and captive breeding. By 2009 the population of oystercatchers had stabilized, and biologists suggest that their numbers may be increasing. With the help of David McLean, I retrace Teale's birding activities and record many of the same species. In just three days we spot sixty-eight kinds of birds. One of my favorites is the black-necked stilt, an extraordinarily tall shorebird perched on long spindly red legs. Amazingly, this bird, quite common on Bulls today, does not appear on Teale's long list.

One morning the "half-buried wreck of a ship—timbers of a rum-runner which went aground"—looms offshore, and "the scattered skeletons of hurricane or storm-blasted trees" block my progress along Boneyard Beach. Further on, I come upon the carcass of a small pilot whale that has washed ashore a day or two ago. Its ebony skin and creamy white underbelly glow in the warm morning light. The massive domed head and brilliant ivory teeth make me think of Melville's Moby Dick. And as I turn to leave, three turkey vultures launch themselves from a nearby tree in anticipation of a feast.

Inland, as Teale noted, wild deer continue to feed in the shadows; raccoons pad along sand paths; black fox squirrels clamor up tree trunks; and a host of alligators, most of them less active than their Okefenokee brethren, lounge beside the ponds. At twilight I continually hear the strange, mechanized refrain of a courting chuck-will's-widow hidden somewhere in a massive live oak beyond my bedroom window. Late that night a storm blows in, knocking out power to the island the following morning. We sit at the kitchen table eating dry cereal and imagining Edwin and Nellie beside us. I set out on a second morning walk, this time headed south along a narrow sand trail. Tree branches shake wildly in the wind, and I'm careful not to touch understory vegetation. Teale "accumulated almost 30 ticks" during one morning walk and reported that Bulls was "one of the most heavily infested spots in the country." These were lone star ticks, prevalent in large numbers but capable of causing little pain. Outdoor enthusiasts today have become more wary of ticks, after people in New England and the Midwest began to complain of headaches, fever, fatigue, and arthritis. In 1980, a spirochete found in blacklegged ticks was identified as the cause of Lyme disease, named for its early appearance in that Connecticut town. The rates of Lyme infection have continued to climb, in large part because "deer" ticks have undergone a population explosion. A friend of mine who hunts in Connecticut encountered hundreds of ticks on his socks and pants within minutes of entering the woods. The bite from just one of these infected ticks, if not detected early, has been linked to symptoms like facial palsy, encephalopathy, and chronic fatigue. Janisse Ray suffered through late stage Lyme disease from a tick bite she never detected. She required bed rest for weeks and intravenous antibiotics, but she still experienced continual headaches. Because blacklegged ticks are making their way south, I follow Teale's protocol and examine myself twice a day on Bulls.

Near Summerhouse Pond lies the "little fenced-in plot lost amid the palms, live oaks, and pines." Four weathered headstones commemorate the Magwood family, renowned oystermen, who once resided on the southern half of Bulls. The tallest stone belongs to James E. Magwood, born 1838, died 1906, the brother of Robert, who purchased a portion of the island in 1882. James and his son Clarence constructed a homestead not far from the southern tip—a brick cistern is apparently all that remains. Clarence's wife, Bessie Viola, occupies a second grave, and close beside her lies the remains of her infant daughter Mildred, who failed to survive her first year. A fourth stone marker commemorates the death of a second child, Claude, who lived from 1882 to 1884.

Although Edwin left no record of his reaction, these graves in this "loneliest cemetery since Marco Island" would undoubtedly have affected him, especially during this first week of April. He and Nellie had received the telegram announcing that their son was missing in action on April 2, 1945. Ever after, as Edwin confessed to his journal, Christmas and Easter "would never be the same again."

This father's letter to his son was penned on April 1: "I imagine this is the strangest Easter Sunday you ever spent.... Wherever you are, you know we love you and wish you all the luck in the world." However, Pfc. David Teale never opened this letter, and it came back to its Baldwin, New York, sender two months later with the envelope stamped "DECEASED."

An only child of parents who were themselves only children, David was especially close to his mother and father. The family often hiked and canoed together, and David had earned the rank of Eagle Scout. Both parents wrote to their son each week after he joined the army in 1942, and in these letters, which David saved, a proud father encourages his eighteen-year-old recruit to improve his spelling and accept the rigors of basic training. David shipped out for Europe the week following Christmas in 1943, and photographs taken before he disembarked show a fine-featured young man with olive skin, oversized ears, and a wide warm smile. He appears more comfortable standing next to his mother.

David's letters home from Europe trace the history of a soldier's maturation. For instance, in November 1944 he is thinking of "the wonderful example of love that was ever before me," and he rejects his mother's comparison. "You know he is a great man . . . and I do not think I could ever be as great as he." A month later the young private engaged the enemy somewhere in France. Shaken by his experience, he writes that he must leave "matters straightened at home." Two painful confessions follow: the "heavy kissing and petting" of a girl named Nancy back home, and his indulgence in "self-abuse known as masturbation" overseas. "I love you all so much that tears almost come when I have to write this to you. However now that it is over I feel much relieved."

On Christmas Eve, David wrote to apologize for mailing "such a letter as I did." Two weeks later, on January 12, his words suggest a new sense of confidence. "Ever since 1945 I have felt like a new man. I think I shed a coat of old evils when I passed the New Year. I feel too that I have grown considerably in all ways." Still hoping to receive a response to his "letter of evils," David tells his father that he has recently joined the Tiger Patrol, a volunteer battalion trained to gather reconnaissance behind enemy lines. Edwin must have pondered what prompted David to volunteer for this dangerous assignment so close to the war's end and whether his lack of response to his son's "letter of evils" might have influenced that decision. The arc from adolescent self-gratification to willing self-sacrifice in the service of others I feel certain crossed this literary father's mind.

On March 15, with Victory Day only two months away, members of the Tiger Patrol were called into action. David volunteered to join eleven other soldiers ordered to pinpoint enemy strength across the Moselle River in preparation for a massive assault. In three rubber rafts, the Patrol crossed into Germany under the cover of darkness and returned to safety. However, when they were ordered back to gain further intelligence, the Germans were waiting. Only four managed to escape the heavy fire and reach the French shore. David Teale was not among those rescued.

It would take Edwin six long months to learn the details of this tragic mission. Ultimately, after numerous requests to the army went unanswered, he took matters into his own hands. Relying on a souvenir flag David had mailed home, Edwin tracked down one of the surviving soldiers and arranged to meet him in Plymouth, Massachusetts. There, at a restaurant near the young man's home, the author learned firsthand the details of his son's death. "How taut and strange a night that was," Edwin recalled in his *North with the Spring* journal, "the questions—the answers—the calmness—the sense of seeing a play with other actors than ourselves."

⟋ ⟋ ⟋

On Easter Sunday I read Teale's letter to my wife, Susie, in bed beside me. We phone our girls, wishing them a happy holiday and sharing our memories of egg hunts, colorful dresses, and baskets filled with chocolates. Susie has taken a week's vacation to join me with four other couples on Fripp Island, a resort destination 60 miles south of Bulls. Here, among manicured golf courses and lavish homes, the signs of spring progress: bluebirds have already nested, ospreys feed their young, and a dozen great egrets jockey for position atop their precarious stick nests.

We walk the beach together that morning, where I tell my wife of a conversation I had in Florida with my closest high school friend, Jeff Hoffman. Jeff's father, Buddy, owned a lumberyard, and one summer during high school I worked there driving a truck. I loved the physicality of that work, as well as my interactions with the carpenters and plumbers. Most of all I looked forward to the end of each day, when Buddy's youngest brother, Sonny, pulled five tall cans of Schaefer beer from a brown paper bag. We sat together in the yard retelling the day's events: the mistakes we made, the customers we ogled, the weekend plans. When I told Jeff how important those conversations had been—my first real exposure to the blue-collar world—he smiled and then recalled how much he had looked forward to sitting down with my parents and discussing ideas and hearing reports from *Scientific American* and the *New York Times*.

Jeff said Buddy had died five years earlier, and it took several years for him to realize how much his dad had shaped his life. Jeff loved to sail in high school, and he had always assumed his mother had talked his father into buying a sailboat. In fact, it was entirely Buddy's idea, although he loved to fish and had no interest in sailing. "In lots of ways like that, without ever taking credit, my dad sensed what might interest me and steered me in those directions."

Our conversation that night ended with Stephen Kochle, a high school friend who was killed at the age of twenty. An only child, Steve lived on my side of town, and I often picked him up on our way to the bars. Reserved, self-disciplined, polite beyond his years, he fell asleep one night driving home alone. I was back at college at the time, and it was Jeff who had called me. We were pallbearers at his funeral, and neither of us could recall much about that ceremony. I reminded Jeff that we had visited Steve's parents after the service. There were six of us packed together in their living room, studying our shoes, searching for words to say how sorry we were.

Looking back, I should have found the courage to speak. I knew his parents better than the others, and I was the only one in the room who wasn't there with him that night. And his folks were desperate for stories about their son. None of us could muster that courage, and after twenty minutes of silence we stood up and left. That hunger in their eyes still haunts me.

Fripp Island is connected to Hunting Island, South Carolina's most popular state park, via a short bridge. Hunting remains largely undeveloped, and its narrow sand trails, cleared by Civilian Conservation Corps recruits in the 1930s, offer splendid paths for birdwatching and bike riding. Pine warblers, American redstarts, hooded warblers, and common yellowthroats flitted through the canopy, and a male painted bunting, a "Nonpareil," visited the park feeder. One afternoon, while riding ahead of others, I slammed on my brakes in time to avoid running headlong over a thick-bodied copperhead sprawled in midpath. The snake, with an exquisite pattern of reddish-brown scales, immediately curled to a tight coil and fixed me with its eyes. Then it relaxed, stretched to full length, and slithered off the trail. On several occasions, Teale had almost stepped on a snake whose "pattern blended perfectly with its background of crisscrossing leaves" on Bulls Island.

During the 1970s, the state dredged an inland lagoon on Hunting Island, a waterway where herons, egrets, osprey, and ducks now nest and feed. I paddled over to Hunting with friends on several occasions and spent hours exploring the shallow byways. At the lagoon entrance, we float past skeletons of storm-wracked beach cottages, reminders of the few families who built here before the state purchased the park. We watched kingfishers hit the water's surface, ospreys bring fish to their young, and a mother otter, her two kits clinging to her back, warily approach. I even glimpsed a massive loggerhead turtle surfacing to breathe among the breakers.

The story of Fripp Island, like its popular cousin Hilton Head, involves an entrepreneur with vision and a thirst for profit. Set apart from the mainland and mostly wooded until the 1960s, Fripp was purchased by Jack Kilgore for $500,000 and connected to Hunting Island via a privately financed bridge. The young developer's plans called for transforming its folded topography and removing most of the pine, live oak, and palmetto forest. Kilgore lured a handful of early investors, installed a first-class golf course, and designed a luxury inn based on a Polynesian theme. More important to its feel today, he established strict covenants mandating single-family dwellings, none of which could exceed two stories, and limiting commercial development to two locations.

I meet Lee at a crabbing platform one morning. He says, "Kilgore invited my father here in 1963. They went over in a boat, and he offered the entire beachfront for $50,000. Course, nobody wanted ocean property at that time." Lee's father paid $5,000 for an acre of woods where his family now vacations in one of the sixteen mushroom-shaped homes known as Bartoli Topsiders that formed the earliest residential community on

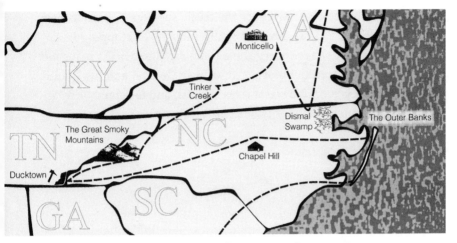

Detail of South and North Carolina and Virginia travels.

the island. These odd octagons appear out of character today beside the sprawling oceanfront mansions with second-floor balconies, multiple decks, and commanding views of the encroaching ocean.

What saved Fripp from the random rapacious development that has ruined much of North and South Carolina's coastline can be traced back to Jack Kilgore's original covenants and to individuals like Lee who were willing to go to court to enforce them. Today, bike paths crisscross the island, and most residents prefer golf carts to cars. Little by little, I come to appreciate the allure of Fripp, especially in my walks after dark. Wisteria and gardenia perfume the evening air, and wetlands reverberate with the din of mating frogs. The click of deer hooves echoes against an empty golf cart path, and further out, a chuck-will's-widow repeats its three-note song. From deep within the swamp a great horned owl hoots. By week's end we have discovered the owl's nest, and we watch as two chicks, almost ready to fledge, hop awkwardly from branch to branch.

As Susie helps me repack the truck, she asks if I plan to visit my father's grave. I hadn't really thought of stopping in Catawba, but she encourages me to do so. She says, "It helps me when I talk to my mother, my Uncle George, and my grandmothers. Your dad was always curious, and he would be interested in hearing about your trip."

The Next Generation

Through an opening in the burlap blind, I saw Cottontail's brown shape leap from the brush pile. She
moved out into the field, her white eartag showing in
the dying light. This time she did not stop to groom
her fur or browse on sumac bark as she usually did
on leaving her bed. Another cottontail had suddenly
appeared, and I saw it follow her.

JOHN K. TERRES, *From Laurel Hill to Siler's Bog*

Edwin Teale followed the contours of the coast into North Carolina, stopping at the edge of a "swamp without standing water," an extensive moist depression with a hardpan base. Here
he found and photographed pitcher plants and Venus flytraps,
odd carnivorous adaptations with eyelash-shaped spines. He
expressed concern that local people were overharvesting and
commercializing these rare and delicate species. I remember
supermarket displays during the 1960s that featured plastic-
lidded tin containers with these tiny green curiosities rooted
in wet sandy soil. I begged my mother to purchase a Venus fly-
trap, and after bringing the plant home, I patrolled the house
in search of flies. The gradual closing of the trap's delicate
"jaws" when I dropped in prey never lost its magic. Teale had
been right, of course, to argue against merchandizing these
rarities, for in less than a month the appendages withered, the

leaves yellowed, and the plant turned brown. I never learned the cause—whether too much water, not enough sun, or some insufficient nutrient was responsible—but Venus flytraps soon disappeared from our house and later from supermarket shelves.

I cross Pamlico Sound via the Cedar Island ferry and access the Outer Banks along the southern tip at Hatteras. Driving through the village brings back additional memories from adolescence, for during one summer my dad had arranged for us to go deep-sea fishing with my cousins. He had booked an oceangoing charter aboard the *Albatross II*, captained by Ernal Foster, the man who introduced sport fishing to the region as early as 1937. Captain Foster, who we immediately nicknamed "the old salty dog," spoke in a dialect none of us could fathom. We pieced together bits of his story on the long ride out to the Gulf Stream—how he had dropped out of school to join the Coast Guard and only later returned home to fish. He had designed his own fishing boat and was the first to charge visitors to sport fish. We spent a fine day trolling for billfish and returned to the dock that afternoon with a load of wahoo, dolphin, mackerel, and tuna.

Unlike my brothers, I continued to share my father's passion for deep-sea fishing. We spent many Saturdays over the next decade standing side by side along headboat rails anchored off Long Island Sound. We chummed for bluefish, jigged for tinker mackerel, set hooks on flounders, and reeled in countless codfish. At times late in the voyage my dad and I appeared to be the only two still manning our reels. Years later, during graduate school, I spent three summers shucking scallops aboard a steel-hulled trawler docked in Wanchese, North Carolina. My father loved to hear my stories of these adventures, of where we fished and what came up in the dredge. He hungered for the ocean, I think, and might well have set off in that direction had his father's early death not burdened him with family responsibilities. Except for our week at Hatteras, we managed only one other fishing adventure as a family—a halibut charter in Alaska's Kenai Peninsula. Here, again, my dad and I pulled in fish while the rest of the family tended to their stomachs.

Teale found his drive across the Outer Banks unsettling: "The isolated shore that had remained so little changed since the days of Sir Walter Raleigh's lost colony had disappeared in a rush of recent construction." The beach houses and hotels he noted—the Wilber Wright, the First Colony, the Shangri-La— "like a long city fronting the sea," have long since vanished, replaced today by even more unsightly concrete monstrosities. Edwin and Nellie found a stretch of beach past Nags Head where they could build a fire and enjoy a picnic lunch.

That 70-mile stretch of sand fronting the Atlantic Ocean near the Coast Guard station where the couple paused continues to be monitored by the National Park Service today. Officers are asked to enforce an increasingly complicated set of policies crafted by focus groups, environmentalists, Virginia Beach off-road enthusiasts, and local fisherman. Five years ago the Defenders of Wildlife and the Audubon Society sued the Park Service for failing to protect nesting shorebirds and sea turtles along this stretch of shore. As a consequence, just two months before I visit, Park Service officials have begun to implement a new management plan: one that calls for 28 miles of beachfront to be set aside for year-round off-road vehicle (ORV) use, another 13 miles for seasonal ORV use, and 26 miles to be designated as vehicle-free areas open only to pedestrians. "Unworkable" and "too complicated" are the words local people use when I ask about the plan.

"Nowhere else in our travels did we come upon change so sweeping," Teale concluded. This discomfort might explain why the couple chose to bypass the nearby Pea Island Wildlife Refuge, a preserve established to protect migrating shorebirds in 1937. I spend a fine afternoon there, walking the boardwalk trails that extend out into the sound and watching long-billed avocets feed along the water's edge. A great blue heron stabs a migrating elver, shakes its bill, and swallows the limp silver ribbon. At the Refuge Visitor Center I strike up a conversation with a pair of amateur birders who volunteer there regularly. Their notes for the weekend of April 10 include the following assortment of birds: 100 black-bellied plovers, 50 avocets, 10 greater yellowlegs, 30 gadwalls, 100 dunlins, 10 green-winged teal, 10 black ducks, 4 white ibis, 6 herring gulls, 1 laughing gull, 2 osprey, 1 snowy egret, 12 great blue herons, and 2 killdeers. All along the coast, it seems, spring's pulse is quickening.

Later that day I turn inland for Chapel Hill, located in the piedmont section of the state, where my predecessor had pored over museum collections, accepted invitations to lecture, and shared meals with colleagues. I harbor other plans, for UNC is my alma mater where I spent eight productive years. Like so many college towns, Chapel Hill has managed to remake itself with every passing decade. A luncheonette with stiff-backed booths, linoleum floor tiles, and waitresses in T-shirts has given way to an upscale tavern with brass railings and hanging ferns. I park on Franklin Street and head for the Louis Round Wilson Library, the building where Teale enjoyed an exhibit focused on sandhill birds. Here, in a spacious reading room, I spent hours poring over Wordsworth, Keats, and Coleridge. On weekends I also read the works of John Burroughs, Aldo Leopold, and John K. Terres, whose volume *From Laurel Ridge to Siler's Bog: The Walking Adventures of a Naturalist* was awarded the John Burroughs nature writing prize in 1971, the year I began my undergraduate career.

"An aspiring nature writer who has shown real ability," Teale wrote after being introduced to John Terres in New York City in 1948. They shared a love for birds, and each had contributed articles to popular natural history magazines. Years later Teale would accept an invitation to write the introduction to Terres' expanded edition of *Songbirds in Your Garden*. Describing the work as "filled with contagious enthusiasm as well as with helpful hints," the older naturalist, with characteristic

Slider and snapping turtle surface at Pea Island National Wildlife Refuge, North Carolina. Photo by author.

diffidence, limits his remarks to the rapid rise of bird feeders rather than detailing his friendship with the author.

Unlike *North with the Spring,* whose audience was familiar with backyard nature, *From Laurel Ridge to Siler's Bog* attempts to appeal to a more urban reader, one out of touch with life on the farm. Terres' chapter-length accounts portray animals as individuals—a female cottontail, a golden mouse, a muskrat family, and the "jet black gobbler of willow oak swamp." Raccoons, hawks, and owls take on distinct personalities based on the author's extensive observations and sympathetic eye. Like Teale he begins the book with a map, but rather than depicting the eastern United States, Terres circumscribes a 2-mile parcel surrounding nearby Mason Farm. And as the opening quote to this chapter illustrates, the author relies on "methods known to hunters and photographers" like live-trapping and ear-tagging to identify his subjects and follow their various activities.

Both Teale and Terres set out to discover the habits of one rarely observed rodent, the golden mouse, a southern tree-climbing species with a red-gold coat, a white underbelly, and delicate pink feet. Teale had hoped to encounter one of these uncommon mice in his travels through the Okefenokee Swamp. Instead, he was forced to content himself with anecdotes offered by Will Cox, the native swamper who had seen a golden mouse leap into the canal and swim across underwater. The closest the couple came to sighting their quarry was finding a "ball of dry vegetation" that served as the creature's nest. Terres, too, discovered a telltale nest, and he was determined to acquaint himself with its occupant. After setting live traps and sprinkling bait, he slept the night in a nearby cot. These efforts paid off, and he not only captured his first golden mouse, but he kept the creature caged for further observation over the next "one hundred and ten days." *From Laurel Ridge to Siler's Bog* includes scenes of the author talking to the mouse as it cracks seeds, relocating the rodent to his New York City apartment, and forcing himself not to handle the creature as it grows ever wilder.

I plan to visit Mason Farm to discover what has changed since Terres sojourned there and to reflect on how nature writing itself has evolved. For assistance I reach out to Johnny Randall, botanical garden assistant director for conservation. Randall knows this property almost as well as Terres did, and as soon as we meet he warns me that the author's hand-drawn map is no longer accurate. In 1984 the University established the Mason Farm Biological Reserve to protect these natural areas and support experiential academic research. However, much of the pastureland Terres depicted has since grown up into brushy thickets, and biological reserve staff are only now beginning to re-create the prairie-like habitats Terres described in *From Laurel Ridge to Siler's Bog.*

Beyond the gate, we pause first at a lonely cemetery beneath a grove of cedar trees. Here lie buried the Reverend James Pleasant Mason and his wife, Mary, along with their two daughters, Mattie and Varina, both of whom died of typhoid fever in their early twenties. I alternate between ruminating on Teale and remembering my own father, who first encouraged me to apply to UNC, his alma mater. He had been desperately lonely when he first arrived at college, as well as unprepared for the rigors of undergraduate work. He described those first months in his autobiography, recalling that the high point of his freshman year was "receiving letters from home, and especially Mother's 'care' packages with their wonderful cookies and homemade candy."

Indigo buntings sing from shrub-tops, and blue grosbeaks, iridescent robin-sized birds I've never seen before, chase one another from tree to tree. We stop to check on a covey of bobwhite quail Randall is raising to reintroduce to a field where Terres often observed them. And we wander beside the banks of Morgan Creek, noting the tracks of muskrats searching for food. We venture into the author's Big Oak Woods, a hardwood bottomland that according to my guide features 300-year-old white oaks. "Barred owls continue to nest in these woods," he assures me, "along with red-tailed hawks and an ever-larger flock of turkeys." At various locations we pause to imagine the solitary Terres—crouched behind his makeshift blind, seated with a flashlight after dark, sleeping out beneath the stars.

The Mason Farm Reserve, like many of the refuges I visit, requires ongoing active management by trained professionals. We walk past one field that was bush-hogged the week before and another where native grasses have been planted following a regimen of fire. Calling attention to these restoration strategies, Johnny Randall emphasizes that such obvious manipulation would have troubled both Terres and Teale. "They came of age when the myth of 'pristine nature' held sway." Any evidence of past human activity was removed wherever possible, and signs of ongoing human interactions with the landscape were carefully concealed. In the past two decades, however, environmental historians led by William Cronon have called attention to the artificiality of this approach. They have encouraged decision-makers to showcase rather than suppress evidence of past human activity. Focusing on the Apostle Islands in his home state of Wisconsin, Cronon argues that "acknowledging past human impacts upon these islands is not to call into question their wildness; it is rather to celebrate, along with the human past, the robust ability of wild nature to sustain itself when people give it the freedom it needs to flourish in their midst."

Celebrating the intersections between man and nature by including stories of logging, hunting, and other forms of resource extraction more accurately portrays the history of a place like Mason Farm, as well as larger refuges like the Everglades and the Okefenokee. Calling attention to patterns of human disturbance in a protected site forces those who visit to relinquish the illusion of a pristine landscape. Furthermore, replacing this myth with a richer and more complicated narrative increases the chance that restoration strategies like William Jordan's might take hold. As J. B. MacKinnon, a proponent of rewilding, has written, "When we choose the kind of nature we will live with, we are also choosing the kind of human beings we will be. We shape the world, and it shapes us in return."

As I leave Chapel Hill, I try to imagine how Teale would have responded to my recent observations. Many details on Bulls Island and in the Okefenokee would have pleased him, for these locations have grown wilder in the intervening years. Trees have put on girth, and once-persecuted animals have returned. At other locations, however, like Wakulla Springs and Corkscrew Swamp, my predecessor would be troubled, for the bird species that triggered these protection efforts have recently disappeared. Teale helped champion many of the successes of the environmental movement throughout the 1970s, a time during which he also feared the threat of nuclear annihilation. The forecast of melting polar ice, species extinction, rising seas, and extreme weather events would, I suspect, engender both nightmares and loud calls for action.

Clouds obscure the morning sun as I drive down Catawba's main street and park at the Methodist cemetery where my father lies buried. The church door is unlocked and I peek inside, recalling his casket draped in flowers and family photos. The service would have pleased him, I think, both because of his sons' testimonials and because a hometown crowd turned out to honor his memory. While I wander the cemetery looking for his stone, I think back on how much he yearned for recognition. I remember one Christmas when he was overseas, helping diagnose tuberculosis in Taiwan, and he sent our girls a copy of Shel Silverstein's *The Giving Tree*. It seemed an odd gesture, and I was embarrassed as I read the book aloud. The boy in the story takes everything from an old apple tree—its fruit, branches, limbs, and trunk—leaving only a severed stump. "Boy, I have nothing left to give" is how I remember the story ending. When I actually looked once more at its final words, they read: "And so the tree was happy."

Red clay still outlines the newly planted grass. I scan the names of those buried beside him—his beloved mother, Catherine, who lived with us for many years, his Uncle John, and his long absent father, William Sr., whose departure shaped my father's course. My dad and I had each in our own awkward way attempted to say how much we appreciated and loved the other.

I lingered for a time beside his grave—reminiscing about Maggie high atop the airboat, Susie walking with friends along the beach, Meade sightseeing in Charleston. I assured my dad that the entire family had pledged to attend the celebration of my mom's ninetieth birthday and that I would stop and check on his farm on my way home. Finally, in remembrance of our times on the ocean together, I placed a shell I'd picked up at Fripp beside his stone.

The Prettiest Shade of Red

We came suddenly on a nightmare region, a land
of death and desolation. The trees disappeared. At
first the great rolling hills supported dead grass and
a few stunted oaks scattered at rapidly widening
distances. Then, even these stunted trees disappeared and mile after mile we drove among bare
slopes where what remained of the broken sod hung
like pieces of hide on the red clay of the exposed
hillsides. . . . Blighted into nightmare form, the
countryside seemed almost lifeless.

EDWIN WAY TEALE, JOURNAL OF *North with the Spring*

Sometimes the experience of a place runs counter to our expectations. Nathaniel Hawthorne best described the difficulty
of reconciling imagination and reality. Before a highly antici-
pated trip to Niagara Falls in September 1832, Hawthorne had
been "haunted with a vision of foam and fury, and dizzy cliffs,
and an ocean tumbling down out of the sky." Yet the reality
failed to gratify his exaggerated desires. "Oh, that I had never
heard of Niagara till I beheld it! Blessed were the wanderers of
old, who heard its deep roar, sounding through the woods, as
a summons to an unknown wonder. . . . Nature has too much
good taste and calm simplicity to realize [my vision]. My mind
had struggled to adapt these false conceptions to the reality,

and finding the effort vain, a wretched sense of disappointment weighed me down."

Driving south toward Ducktown, Tennessee, I harbored my
own vision of nature in extremis. I prepared myself for a modern-day wasteland: the site of a defunct copper mine that had
been in continuous operation for 140 years. My expectations
were based on the vivid portrait Teale had penned in the epigraph above. As I turned off Interstate 68 east of Chattanooga
where the borders of Tennessee, Georgia, and North Carolina intersect, I saw no evidence of the "stunted trees . . . bare
slopes . . . and eroded hillsides" my predecessor had described.
Following signs for the Ducktown Basin Museum, I felt instead
the warmth of April sunlight filtered through pine boughs and
glimpsed robins hopping across green lawns. The museum
site, now owned by the Tennessee Historical Commission and
listed on the National Registry of Historic Places, is situated
in a residential neighborhood at the top of a long winding
hill. A number of abandoned structures remain, including the
Hoist House that once protected the engines used to raise and
lower men and equipment into the Burra Burra mine, as well
as a smaller Boiler House, where steam was produced to power
these hoists. What had served as the mine office headquarters
until 1975 now houses the museum's extensive collection.

Originally forest, the land surrounding Ducktown held copper ore beneath its surface. From 1843 until 1900, thick black
clouds of sulfur dioxide, a by-product of the primitive roasting
process that consumed the trees and purified the copper, continually wafted across Ducktown basin. Mixed with water, this
noxious smoke formed sulfuric acid, a poison so potent that it
scorched the land, killing shrubs, grasses, eventually the soil
itself. By the turn of the twentieth century, this "wasteland,"
some 36 square miles in area, had become the largest man-
made biological desert in the nation.

The museum's docent, Dawna Standridge, a short, silver-
haired woman with a pleasant smile, informs me that her

father and husband both worked in the mines. She continues to live in one of the houses Teale characterized as "pink with red dust," homes financed by the mining company and later sold to a handful of fortunate employees. A miner's life was hard, although, according to my guide, her father enjoyed the work, "especially in winter—where the underground·mine stayed a constant 72 degrees." Light was important to this community, and one wall of the museum depicts the evolution of the miner's helmet from raccoon fat to the electric battery. Another exhibit attempts to re-create the experience of the underground mine, offering a claustrophobic chamber where a dimly lit mannequin holds a pneumatic drill. I found the deep silence in that dark closet somehow reassuring.

Along with tools and rock samples illustrating varying amounts of copper ore, the display cases include early photographs of the copper basin, some taken by Marion Post Wolcott in the late 1930s. Wolcott's distant panoramas highlight a satin skin, bathed in sienna, burnt ocher, and oxblood, with spidery veins that trace dark patterns of eroded soil. They document a realm of perpetual twilight, a surreal landscape that reminds me of images sent back from the moon. Here I can see not only Teale's nightmare vision but also the otherworldly beauty that once drew visitors from miles away.

Like mining communities everywhere, Ducktown had its share of controversy. There had been occasional labor strikes, and my guide remembers her father instructing her not to associate with the children of scabs. And there were lawsuits, mostly brought by those who lost their ability to raise cattle or grow crops. Tennessee's courts initially ruled that mining profits and community well-being superseded the interests of outlying farmers, and so, although individuals were compensated for damages, injunctions to close the mines repeatedly failed. Then, in 1905 the state of Georgia took its case against the Tennessee copper mines to the U.S. Supreme Court. The high court ruled that mining companies were, in fact, liable

"Broken sod hung like pieces of hide on the red clay." Photo by E. W. Teale. Edwin Way Teale Papers, Archives and Special Collections at the Thomas J. Dodd Research Center, University of Connecticut Libraries. Used with permission.

for the noxious smoke that crossed state lines, and the justices instructed mine owners to develop and deploy methods to capture sulfur dioxide or cease operations. As a result, from 1907 onward, sulfuric acid, in addition to copper, formed a significant by-product from Ducktown basin. Teale had driven past the great smelter in the heart of the desert, with its "lofty stacks discharging their fumes high in the air above."

Today the air looks clear, and the smelting operations have disappeared. Wandering outside the museum, I look down on a collapsed and flooded portion of the mine encircled by a chain link fence. Three hundred and fifty feet below lay a pool of water stained turquoise by constant contact with the

View across Burra Burra Copper Mine in 2012. Photo by author.

remaining copper ore. The sterile legacy of the Burra Burra mine, though less obvious, is nonetheless evident from this vantage: pale tufts of grass sprout from the raw red clay and spindly shrubs with yellow-green leaves offer only a hint of shade. The U.S. Forest Service purchased much of the basin when the ore played out, and it established a CCC camp in the 1930s that attempted reclamation without much success. Teale was not optimistic that "this moonscape [could] ever be made fertile again," and his chapter "The Poisoned Hills" served as a paradigm for careless ignorance regarding man's use of toxic chemicals more than a decade before the appearance of *Silent Spring*.

Not until the 1980s were ecologists, aided by technology, gradually able to enrich the soils using specialized bacteria, acid-hardy legumes, a regimen of fertilizers, and aerial re-seeding. Little by little nature has reestablished its tenuous foothold, and today many of the 16 million pine trees planted around Ducktown have begun to thrive. Attempts to purify the water in the nearby North Potato and Davis Mill Creeks have proven more challenging, for studies conducted in the 1970s indicated that only one aquatic organism, an insect species, remained alive. In 2001 the Environmental Protection Agency, the Tennessee Department of Environment and Conservation, and OXY USA (a subsidiary of Occidental Petroleum Corporation) agreed to work together to clean up contaminated water. Their ongoing plan includes removing wastes, installing surface caps as well as collection systems, and revegetating holding ponds with native grasses. They have also refurbished a treatment plant, responsible for removing 19 million pounds of metals and neutralizing 41 million pounds of acid from Davis Mill Creek alone. Future efforts include continued surface water cleanup and the installation of an interpretive recreational trail system.

Before departing, Teale noticed ants scurrying beneath his feet. When he placed a thermometer beside the anthill, the temperature rose to 115 degrees. Without the shade of green plants, the sun beat down relentlessly, baking this parched earth. Today children who live in Ducktown can walk to school along shaded sidewalks and chase one another across grassy parks. They are able to hike to the summits of once-eroded hills, ride a zip line stretched across the valley, or experience some of the finest white-water rafting anywhere in Tennessee. In fact, unless they visit the Ducktown Mining Museum, most residents have no inkling that their home ground was once scarred and poisoned beyond recognition.

I watch a swallowtail butterfly glide up and over the barbed wire fence where I stand, and I count two dozen robins clustered beside an enormous pot on the museum grounds. It once functioned as a ladle for handling molten copper. When I step inside to thank Dawna for her tour, her final comment turns my expectations on their head. "It used to be a pretty sight, you know, especially at sunrise and sunset. Those deep red hills surrounding just glowed. Back then we had no rats, no snakes, no bugs in town. Just that prettiest shade of red."

◢ ◢ ◢

Ducktown offered the most dramatic example of landscape restoration I encountered on my trip. Time and technology have revitalized a once poisoned land. Since Teale's era copper mining has migrated west, where concerns focus mainly on disposal of mine tailings and the enormous volume of water the process consumes. However, unprecedented landscape degradation continues across the southern United States in the form of mountain-top removal in search of coal. Hollows in West Virginia and Kentucky have been obliterated, streams poisoned, and whole communities destroyed. And thanks to industry lobbying, the most horrific of these sites have been declared off-limits, even to passing airplanes.

Another more sinister tool of extraction has begun to worry environmentalists from New York to North Carolina. Hydraulic fracturing, designed to extract natural gas from massive underground shale beds, also threatens to poison the earth. Fracking, as it has come to be known, relies on millions of gallons of water laced with chemicals like methanol, naphthalene, benzene, sulfuric acid, and formaldehyde, injected under high pressure into horizontal wells. Gas companies have successfully lobbied to avoid disclosing the complete list of chemicals, and thanks to the George W. Bush administration, they also claim exemptions to the Safe Drinking Water Act and the Clean Air and Clean Water Acts. There are currently more than 400,000 natural gas wells across the country, and to date there have been over 1,000 complaints regarding tainted water, severe illness, livestock death, and fish kills. Whether fracking produces long-term human health risks is the subject of intense ongoing litigation, and several states, including North Carolina, are embroiled in legal and legislative battles to determine the scope and degree of disclosure that gas companies should be required to provide. In the meantime, environmental researchers are attempting to assess the integrity of wastewater holding ponds and to analyze the resilience of cement casings fashioned to facilitate the removal of tainted water from these wells. The results of these tests, conducted for the most part without the support of the gas industry, are critical given projections that over 60 percent of America's energy will come from natural gas by 2035.

In addition to the Ducktown desert, Edwin and Nellie toured Tennessee's Nickajack Cave on two occasions. Here, in a place where "calendars are meaningless," the couple floated on an underground river and trained a flashlight on the "wheeling forms" of thousands of circling bats. Teale devoted several paragraphs to describing two populations of Nickajack's flying mammals: one that arrived in October and departed in May, and another that included four species that lived here during the summer. Thousands of tiny squeaks given off by these creatures generated a "metallic, grating, high-pitched . . . sizzling sound."

The majority of caves and caverns on public land across the South and Northeast have been declared off-limits to visitors since 2008 in an effort to reduce the spread of white-nose syndrome, a devastating disease that has decimated populations of eastern bats. This fungus, an invasive brought over from Europe, grows at low temperatures and spreads rapidly between bats. Infected animals exhibit unusual behaviors, like flying during the daytime and clustering near the cave entrance during cold winter months. Some bat experts speculate that the fungus eats away at the animal's skin; others believe that it dehydrates the hibernating mammals, which then attempt to leave the cave in search of water. Once introduced, the fungus takes over, in some cases killing 95 percent of the overwintering colony. Nine bat species in twenty-two states have been struck by white-nose syndrome, and five of these, especially the common little brown bat that once frequented Nickajack, have suffered catastrophic mortality. Latest estimates put the total number of bats killed by the fungus between 5.7 and 6.7 million. Farmers are especially likely to feel the impact of these losses as insect pests multiply.

Bats, honeybees, and many species of amphibians have suffered inexplicable recent declines. In the *Sixth Extinction*, Elizabeth Kolbert traces the disappearance of the Panamanian golden frog. Once again an exotic fungus, known as Bd, is believed to be responsible for the near extinction of this once common Central American species. "Today, amphibians enjoy the dubious distinction of being the world's most endangered class of animals." Scientists point to technological innovations in global transport—"during any given twenty-four hour period, . . . ten thousand different species are being moved around the world just in ballast water"—as one likely cause, and a growing number of environmentalists are demanding greater scrutiny and tighter controls on the importation and exportation of plants and animals. Many European countries support a strategy that has come to be known as the precautionary principle, although we in the United States continue to put our faith in more and better technology.

Perhaps the most extreme example of America's technological hubris has arisen in a new field called geoengineering. Proponents of this technology have devised a number of scenarios for combating climate change by cooling the planet in the decades ahead. These fall into two major categories: solar radiation management techniques and atmospheric carbon dioxide removal. On the radiation front, computer modeling suggests that "heating associated with a doubling of CO_2 could be neutralized by deflecting about 1.5 to 2.0 percent of the sum total of the sun's energy currently striking Earth." To accomplish such a task, engineers have suggested launching huge sunshades into the stratosphere or designing what they call "cloud brightening" chambers. Mechanical fountains that float across the ocean would inject microscopic droplets of seawater into passing overhead clouds. The salt in the seawater would then act as a "cloud condensation nuclei," and because the particles that form around these droplets would be infinitesimally smaller than droplets naturally occurring, these seeded clouds would grow slightly but significantly brighter. According to John Latham, one of the leading proponents of this technology, "to completely compensate for a doubling of CO_2, about 50 to 70 percent of the clouds that cover the world's oceans would have to be brightened." For those who favor the other path, removing carbon, their best hope seems to rest with dumping tons of iron filings across a wide area of the ocean to trigger massive plankton blooms that will then absorb large quantities of CO_2.

As one might expect, there is already considerable debate over the feasibility of these technological fixes in the near and long term. According to one group of scientists, "feasibility does not necessarily mean practicality." To date, a majority of the environmental community has counseled caution, reminding enthusiasts that solar radiation management can at best only "reduce the planet's fever for a period, perhaps allowing time for the real roots of climate change to be tackled." Furthermore, either one of these scenarios raises the specter of catastrophic destruction reminiscent of that period in history when the atomic bomb cast its dark shadow. The new list of fears includes not only the development of weapons and the inability to ensure safe uses of this technology but also the chance for miscalculation leading to a climatic collapse.

Atop Clingmans Dome

Every leaf was dripping; every tree trunk was hoary
with moss and lichens. The trees were trees of the
North—spruce and fir and yellow birch. Beneath
them, extending in waves over rocks, over moldering
trunks, over the path before us, was a thick plush
carpet of russet-green moss. We moved down this
cushioned trail as silent as the fog.

EDWIN WAY TEALE, *North with the Spring*

Entering an old-growth forest is like "walking into a cathedral from a city street." Most big trees in the Appalachian
Mountains had been harvested decades before Teale visited;
however, one impressive stand survives in North Carolina's
Nantahala National Forest. Painted trillium, bloodroot, Solo-
mon's seal, and Dutchman's breeches—their white and yellow
flowers vivid in the morning light—carpet the slopes of the
Joyce Kilmer-Slickrock Wilderness when I arrive. Dedicated to
Kilmer, the author of the poem "Trees," who was killed in action in World War I, this last remaining 3,800-acre parcel of
old growth includes 100-foot-tall yellow poplars with 20-foot
circumferences and bark plates as thick as my hand. The se-
cluded hillside, purchased from the Gannett Lumber Company
in 1936, also features old-growth beech, sycamore, red oak,
basswood, and yellow birch. Christopher Camuto, who spent a

decade in the Great Smoky Mountains tracking the reintroduction of endangered red wolves, wondered about this parcel's history and interviewed several residents who knew it from their youth. One of these mountain people, Oleta Nelms, recalled the grove before the chestnut blight arrived. "The woods had a different look back then, a richer shine, a glistening color when the chestnuts got old and spread their crowns. When they died, the limbs fell off the trees, then the bark fell off and the wind rocked them down, and the tulip trees and the hemlocks grew so large as they are now."

Writer Gerald Thurmond visited this forest a decade ago and discovered an immense poplar with an opening in its trunk. Without bending over, he stepped inside: "I extend my arms fully out and spin around without touching the sides of the hollowed bole. As far as I can see above there is space and darkness." Thurmond's description includes huge hemlocks that once rivaled the poplars in circumference and canopy height. Unfortunately, the majority of these magnificent trees have succumbed to the hemlock woolly adelgid, an invasive insect that is changing the landscape of western North Carolina and Tennessee. Because these 17,000 acres are part of a federally designated wilderness, chain saws were not an option for felling dead trees. Using a novel approach, Forest Service staff strapped and detonated dynamite at the base of each diseased and dying hemlock. The resulting grove appears as if a powerful windstorm had swept through, picking off only the conifers. Shattered trunks lie covered in shade, while members of the warbler wave flit from branch to branch.

"Nothing in the world is more alive than a warbler in the spring," Teale had written, and mid-April signals the height of their migration. I inch forward a step at a time at Joyce Kilmer, craning my neck to identify these sparks of vivid color—a sizzle of yellow between poplars, a flash of red perched in a sycamore. "Myrtles, magnolias, Maryland yellowthroats, prairies, and black-and-whites darted . . . or flicked" when Edwin and

Nellie were there. I work to name some of these same species, constrained by the paradox that Jonathan Rosen recognized: "You need to be out in nature, and yet you are dependent on technology—binoculars—and also on the guidebook in your back pocket, which tells you what you're seeing." When I meet a fellow birder strolling with his grandson, he tells me to be on the lookout for a hooded warbler in the poplar trees ahead. The ten-year-old, itching to move on, asks if I've seen any snakes.

I stop for lunch at the Nantahala Outdoor Center, a sprawling complex located beside a river devoted to white-water rafting and competitive kayaking. Begun in 1972, this operation, which has spawned more than a dozen imitators throughout the Gorge, brings more than 500,000 visitors to the Nantahala River to enjoy white water each year. I walk between racks of T-shirts and hats, contemplating the history of this once-wild river. Here, in the spring of 1775, William Bartram, walking alone, met the legendary Cherokee chief Attakullaculla. In perfect English, for he had spent time in London, the chief welcomed the traveler "as a friend and brother." This river has since been "humanized," according to author Rick Bass: "It's a funny river . . . a little sad, really. It's been dammed, for power, but each day it's released for twelve hours to keep the lake behind the dam from flooding. . . . For twelve hours it's a meek and mild trickle . . . for the other twelve hours it's a wild thing, much wilder than it would be if it were free all the time instead of being cooped up half the day." Adventure recreation was in its infancy during Teale's day, and I suspect that his reaction to it would be mixed. Delight that white water could interest so many—and disgust that commercial exploitation has whitewashed nature.

The next morning I set out to follow my predecessor's route to the summit of Clingmans Dome, the tallest peak in the Great Smoky Mountains National Park. Along the same paved road switch-backing up the mountain, I pass shadbush in full bloom and marvel at the variety of trees, plants, mosses, and lichens

Teale once witnessed. An ascent to the Dome in April offers "the equivalent of moving backward more than a month in time or jumping northward more than half a thousand miles in space." Filtered sunlight highlights the steep, half-mile paved trail to the summit, where constant wind gusts have produced an elfin forest. From an earlier observation tower, razed in 1950, Edwin looked out across the high ridge-top, "home to the richest flora and most luxuriant deciduous forests on the North American continent." As the chapter epigraph suggests, the scene before him was lush and verdant.

The luxury of that forest has since departed, and in its place shimmers ghostly trunks of Fraser firs, "bleak as bones," according to Chris Camuto. A tiny invasive insect, the balsam woolly adelgid, which arrived in the United States from Europe in the early 1900s, is largely responsible for the death of these trees. Today, 95 percent of the Fraser firs in the Great Smoky Mountains have succumbed to this invader, and the remaining high elevation ecosystem is drier, more prone to fire, and now blanketed in hip-high seedlings that without treatment will slowly wither as they mature.

National Forest personnel sought to limit the adelgid outbreak in 1996 by spraying insecticidal soap on a 15-acre plot at the summit of Clingmans Dome. To my eye, there is little evidence that the treatment has made any difference. Entomologist Scott Costa at the University of Vermont is exploring another method to combat the adelgids' spread. Costa and his colleagues have had success limiting insect damage by mixing droplets of whey, a by-product of cheese-making, with an insect-killing fungus. Where they have sprayed this biodegradable solution on affected trees in Tennessee, the adelgid growth rate has been reduced by 50 percent. Costa is confident that much of the hemlock and fir forest in the Northeast can be saved or restored by using this alternative to chemical pesticides.

Observation tower atop Clingmans Dome in the Great Smoky Mountain National Forest. Photo by author.

In addition to the adelgid, these summits are affected by toxic smoke from coal-fired power plants, which give the Smokies the distinction of having the worst air quality of any national park. The red spruce and Fraser firs at this elevation are relics of the last ice age and are therefore adapted to cold temperatures and moist conditions. April 2012 marked the end of the warmest twelve-month period since 1895, and climatologists predict that average temperatures in the Southeast will rise 4 to 6 degrees by 2050. As temperatures rise, the fine droplets from fog and light rain—which now account for the 58–60 inches of smokelike precipitation (hence the mountains' name)—will evaporate in the air and fail to reach the ground.

Before retracing my steps back down the concrete spiral platform that has replaced the earlier wooden tower, I meet a man and his son who ask me to take their picture. The boy's father positions them looking out toward the west, a pose he and his father apparently held some twenty-five years ago. When I hand the camera back to him, he seems delighted with the scene in the viewfinder. I wonder if he, or perhaps his son, will notice the blighted background when they place the photos side by side.

In the not-so-distant future, according to Eric Hanson, a writer for *Outside Magazine,* tourists may record a similar scene without leaving the parking lot. Hanson purchased a camera-equipped unmanned aerial vehicle (UAV) and tested his new technology at Clingmans Dome. He flew the drone to the height of the observation deck and held it there until sightseers detected a telltale buzz. To his astonishment they "raised their cameras, tablets, and phones," and after photographing the strange craft, they clapped. Hanson went on to fly his camera at other national parks, and along the way he asked visitors and park managers their opinions about the aerial intruder. Reactions were mixed, and at the present time no rules exist to prohibit unmanned flights over wildlife sanctuaries. Hanson ends his article with this stark declaration: "We should ban the use of drones in all federal wilderness areas immediately." Thinking back on my pleasant hours of solitude at Hells Bay, Minnie's Lake, and Boneyard Beach, I couldn't agree more.

The Appalachian Trail ascends Clingmans Dome, and for the next several hours I hike in Teale's footsteps toward Silers Bald. The sky remains clear, and below me shadbush petals dance in the wind like snowflakes. Yellow dandelions dot the margins of the trail, packed tight in the center from thousands of boots. This popular footpath remained incomplete during Teale's era, as private mountaintop development held it hostage. Finally, in 1968 Lyndon B. Johnson signed into law the National Trails System Act, a statue that created a new class of public lands—national scenic trails—with the Appalachian and the unfinished Pacific Crest Trail as its first designees. The following decade witnessed a surge in the number of backpackers, and the Appalachian Trail has remained the iconic footpath east of the Mississippi ever since. More than 2 million people visit some portion of the Appalachian Trail annually, and of those, less than 1,000 complete the arduous thru-hike from Georgia to Maine.

✶ ✶ ✶

Edwin spent a rare night without Nellie, as he and a colleague hiked to the summit of Mount LeConte. The cabins they occupied in 1947 are still available to hikers who reserve them today. A driving rainstorm greeted the pair the next morning, and their foray down the mountain tested the stamina of these middle-aged naturalists. I elect to drive through rain clouds looking for a place to sleep that evening. My map indicates a small state park located far off the highway. The sites here are primitive: a picnic table and fire ring, a hand pump for water, a single composting toilet, and a metal tube where I deposit my $10 payment. I circle the tight loop at 10 mph and choose a site beside the designated ranger and a safe distance from the four mud-stained pickup trucks piled high with beer cans. Sounds of a late-night party blend with driving rain.

The next morning I build a fire, and the smell of wood smoke, the sight of lilac buds, and the warble of a bluebird make me nostalgic for my New Hampshire home. I decide to forego LeConte, Blowing Rock, and the Greer Drug Company in Lenoir. Instead, I load up on supplies in the village of Cherokee, a tacky tourist town filled with cheap motels, Indian souvenir shops, and abandoned trailers. Edwin used the phrase "suspended animation" to describe the endless hours he spent looking through a windshield. The moment I enter the Blue Ridge Parkway, the numbness of highway miles dissolves. Billboards disappear, together with the flotsam of modern highway culture—fast food restaurants, gasoline stations with digital price boards, overhead wires, and traffic exchanges. Designed as a "museum of the managed American countryside," the Blue Ridge auto road, begun in 1935, was not completed until 1987, when the Linn Cove Viaduct was installed around Grandfather Mountain. This two-lane parkway, with its split rail fences and 100 scenic overlooks, covers 469 miles from its southern entrance in the Smoky Mountains to its northern terminus in Virginia's Shenandoah National Park. Rising over 6,000 feet in elevation, the Blue Ridge forms the highest parkway in the eastern United States. "It is the first use of the parkway idea, purely and wholeheartedly for the purposes of tourist recreation distinguished from the purposes of regional travel," wrote Stanley Abbott, the visionary landscape architect who guided its design. Even Bill Bryson, in his search across America, was stunned by the distinctive beauty of this roadway.

"By now we could close our eyes and see streaming toward us concrete roads, asphalt roads, gravel roads, shell roads, dirt roads," Teale lamented as he and Nellie added Skyline Drive to their compendium of thoroughfares. For me, the rolling hills and wooded valleys—dotted with the pink of mountain laurel, the white of shadbush, the yellow of forsythia, and the earliest azaleas—illustrate the "parks within parks" Stanley Abbott had designed. I stop to tour the Mabry gristmill, built in the first decade of the twentieth century and restored to working order in 1942. Here water splashes down a long wooden trough, while inside the mill, a century-old silence fills the sun-drenched room.

What a noble project it would be to extend this scenic highway from Maine to Florida, creating a companion pathway to the Appalachian Trail and highlighting the observational techniques of Edwin and Nellie Teale. The parkway might even be dedicated in their honor. Traveling less than 40 mph, stopping frequently to check field guides and chat with fellow travelers, sightseers would once again acquaint themselves with the flora and fauna along the way. This pace of travel, once popular in Europe, might help rekindle that civic-minded spirit Americans demonstrated during Franklin Delano Roosevelt's tenure. Given our challenge to reduce greenhouse gases, this parkway of the future might require hybrid autos and feature biofuel buses or slow-moving solar-powered trains.

Jefferson's Phoebe

> A robin had built its nest at the top of one of the col-
> umns of the house on the garden side, and a phoebe
> had its nest on a beam of the carriage house. It
> landed on a wire along which a vine was running,
> balancing itself and bobbing its tail at the same time
> its bright eyes kept us under close surveillance. It
> would dart out and then return again. How many
> robin generations, how many phoebe generations
> have known Monticello as their home.
>
> EDWIN WAY TEALE, JOURNAL OF *North with the Spring*

Annie Dillard turned two in Pittsburgh as Edwin and Nellie Teale worked their way across western Virginia. Twenty-
seven years later her book *Pilgrim at Tinker Creek* would bring
national attention to this rural landscape. Dillard attended
Hollins College, where she studied Thoreau and married her
English professor. She then set to work exploring the hills and
streams surrounding Roanoke, Virginia. Like many other readers, I had been struck when I encountered her voice in 1974:
"I am an explorer then, and I am also a stalker, or the instrument of the hunt itself. . . . I am the arrow shaft, carved along
my length by unexpected lights and gashes from the very sky,
and this book is the straying trail of blood." At a time when
her contemporaries followed in the shadow of Rachel Carson,

Annie Dillard used science, metaphysics, and theology to bear witness to the beauty and terror of the natural world.

Dillard repeatedly quotes from the works of Edwin Way Teale. She is especially drawn to his *Strange Lives of Familiar Insects*, a volume she confesses she "couldn't live without." His stories of monstrous insects like the African Hercules beetle, the clothes moth, ichneumon flies, and the South American honey ant offered lessons in entomology, while other members of his bizarre menagerie such as horsehair worms and migrating eels were "never far from [her] mind." Dillard staunchly resisted the label of nature writer when her book appeared, arguing instead that her literary forays into the natural world were in service of larger questions about man's place in a universe powered by mystery and death.

Aligning herself with those who remain restless for experience, the narrator of *Pilgrim at Tinker Creek* probes with dizzying relentlessness. Her chapters call attention to what we often miss—the intricacy, uncertainty, and drama of the present moment fully lived. "There is always an enormous temptation . . . to diddle around making itsy-bitsy friends and meals and journeys," she warns the reader, "to step aside from the gaps where the creeks and winds pour down, saying, I never merited this grace." Dillard won't have it. "The world is wilder than that in all directions, more dangerous and bitter, more extravagant and bright." Her work, which explores the boundary between mysticism and theology, also straddles the contested territory between fiction and nonfiction. Soon after the book's success, Dillard admitted that its memorable opening scene— where a fighting tomcat she claims as her own kneads her bare chest with its bloody paws—was borrowed (with permission) from a former graduate student. Teale, true to form, wrote to a friend that he could not support *Tinker Creek* for the John Burroughs Prize because it contained too many factual errors.

I'd been forewarned to be on my guard when I arrived in Roanoke—"suburbs flank either side of the Creek," one faculty member had e-mailed, and the university librarian confided that Dillard "employed a good bit of poetic imagination in the book." Nonetheless, I set out to follow Tinker Creek through campus in yet another steady drizzle. Sliding down banks covered in honeysuckle and wild hawthorn, I encountered the creek and attempted to study its surface. "The future is the light on the water; it comes, mediated, only on the skin of the real and present creek." The subject that day was swollen, and the light from its surface reflected a gun-metal gray.

"Big trees stir memories," Dillard had written, and the tall sycamores leaning out over Tinker Creek brought to mind my lost days along Opossum Creek, a stony channel near my aunt and uncle's retreat in rural Pennsylvania. Late on quiet summer afternoons, I delighted in slipping away, rolling up my pant legs, and entering the water. Hunting crayfish had possessed me as muskrats occupied Dillard. I turned over stone after stone, watching for the water to clear. The tiny crustaceans that inhabited the creek bed made their home beneath rocks, and catching them required both patience and speed. Hour after hour I patrolled the shallow stream, hefting rocks, reading sediments, studying the slightest movement behind a curtain of silt. Eventually, when I stood up and straightened my back, a flooded cemetery of tipped-up stones greeted my glance downstream.

Pilgrim at Tinker Creek offers excellent advice on the skill of stalking, on how to empty oneself and thereby go calm. Dillard perfected her technique by pursuing muskrats, those rodents that, like beavers, feed in the evening and have limited eyesight. With practice, she was able to approach a muskrat to within arm's length. John Terres also pursued muskrats in *From Laurel Ridge to Siler's Bog*, although his method of observation was far more intrusive. He drifted across the pond at Mason Farm shining a flashlight in the direction of a splash. Like Dillard, Terres returned again and again until he could identify individual muskrats and follow the progress of a family of seven. What for Terres was scientific inquiry was for Dillard sheer sport. "In a rush of such pure energy I thought I would not need to breathe for days." She wrote to awaken an audience lulled to sleep by endless facts. With chapter titles like "The Horns of the Altar" and "Heaven and Earth in Jest," Dillard hurls her reader headlong into the terror and beauty of the nearby natural world.

Teale, Terres, and Dillard all borrow from Thoreau a seasonal scaffolding on which to organize their insights. Dillard and Terres begin their experiments in January and conclude their meditations in December. However, while the author of *From Laurel Ridge* recorded facts in the service of natural history, Dillard chose a path of exuberant exaggeration. "I preserve the illusion that what is happening on Tinker Creek is the very newest thing, that I'm at the very vanguard and cutting edge of each new season. I don't want the same season twice in a row." I can almost hear Edwin Teale's groan of repudiation, for his four-month journey following spring illustrated that no two seasons are ever the same.

The muddy swirls of Tinker Creek on this day carry sticks, leaves, and Styrofoam cups under roadway bridges and through backyard neighborhoods. I wander back to the Hollins College library, wishing that the author might have served as my guide. Nonetheless, following the creek has helped me comprehend the differences between Dillard and her predecessors. Nature served as her vehicle in pursuit of larger literary aims. Tinker Creek stands in for time itself, and stalking becomes a metaphor for spiritual enlightenment. Ultimately, the pilgrim and the naturalist seek different truths.

*   *   *

I arrive at Monticello, Jefferson's magnificent estate, a full nineteen days ahead of Teale. I want to compare in detail the record of spring's advance between 1947 and 2012. I'm also growing weary of life on the road, and I've begun to yearn for the familiar signs of spring at home. I've missed the sap flow in February, the din of peepers in March, and the courtship of bluebirds, my favorites, in early April. Tree swallows have likely begun to circle our backyard pond. My desire for the comforts of home was exacerbated in part by the upscale "campground" outside of Roanoke where I spent the night. Hot showers, laundry facilities, lighted pathways, and comfortable porch rockers pull me northward.

The long, winding road to Jefferson's hilltop mansion recalls the Blue Ridge Parkway, and hundreds of cars have already parked by 10 a.m. I purchase the $24 ticket and bypass the gift shop to join a vanload of pilgrims, most of whom are middle-aged. Our docent, a pleasant and knowledgeable woman in her mid-fifties, tells us of the struggle Jefferson endured to balance his remarkable talents and complete his ideal home. As the platoon of tourists ahead of us steps in, we ready ourselves for the threshold, where columns and a Palladian dome seem perfectly fitted to their surroundings. Inside the entrance hall, hand-drawn maps, animal skins, Indian artifacts, and fossil bones immediately seem familiar. I've been inside Monticello once before. My family must have visited here in the early 1960s, before the education center and gift shop were installed. My dad's love of history carried us up and down the east coast—to Valley Forge, Gettysburg, colonial Williamsburg, and as I now realize to Jefferson's Virginia.

The former president's collection of gadgets—a time keeping instrument, polygraph, the desk he engineered, and a hidden dumbwaiter—all bring back my adolescent fascination with wooden toys and model airplanes. I marvel now at the polished floors, arched entryways, splendid artwork, and control of natural light. When we reach the tearoom, however, I'm restless to be outdoors, and as the tour concludes, I approach two young women kneeling beside a massive tree stump. The tall, broad-shouldered blonde, who introduces herself as Debbie Donley, marvels as I read a paragraph penned by Teale. An amateur birder herself, Debbie tells me that the phoebe he describes in the chapter epigraph has already begun her nest. "And yesterday I noticed a bluebird coming out of its hole in a cellar support." She points to the carriage house, where I watch the phoebe, its long tail bobbing, perch along the wire and flit toward the sill.

Debbie points out other bird arrivals, and we share phoebe stories. Twice I have interrupted their nesting: once when I filled our barn with smoke by pulling the barbeque grill out of the rain, and a second time when a disoriented mother bird became trapped in the house after dark. We found her dead on the windowsill days later. "How many phoebe generations have known Monticello as their home!" Edwin exclaimed. And how many more generations have lived here since! Almost all the birds he listed had returned to Monticello by April 20. English sparrows, wood thrushes, brown thrashers, mourning doves, catbirds, cedar waxwings, tufted titmice, chickadees, mockingbirds, and orioles—all were here. Strolling the grounds, I notice three additional species Teale had recorded using Jefferson's terminology—"the lettuce bird or goldfinch; the Virginia nightingale or cardinal; and the fieldfare of Carolina or the robin." Turkey vultures sail overhead as I make my way to Jefferson's gravesite, and another birder tells me that a bald eagle has already nested on a power pole three miles away.

The flower gardens too have exploded into bloom. Dogwoods, columbines, redbuds, snowball bushes, and azaleas all show full color, along with purple lilacs, tulips, iris, Scotch broom, Virginia bluebells, and white violets. In addition, I note primrose, bachelor buttons, larkspur, periwinkle, snapdragons, and sweet William in various stages of flowering. Jefferson kept his own book of gardening facts, and among his entries are the following observations: "March 29, 1774 peach trees in bloom—May 4 blue ridge mountains covered in snow, near half fruit of every kind killed"; "April 1, 1782 jonquil and hyacinth in bloom—April 20, tulip and iris bloom"; "March 20,

1794 peaches blossom—April 8, peaches killed"; "May 16, 1811 strawberries come to table." Apple trees have shed their blossoms, and the linden, copper beech, European larch, tulip poplar, and sugar maples that Teale recorded all show leaves. His surmise that these trees were alive during the years in which "the author of the Declaration of Independence was evolving and strengthening his own eloquent philosophy of justice and human rights" has been rebuked in the intervening decades. Core samples reveal that only a single cedar, a species much smaller than its neighboring giants, actually survives from the early 1800s.

The former president's reputation as a champion of human rights has likewise undergone an unfavorable reappraisal. Scholar Annette Gordon-Reed amassed evidence in the early 1990s to support the allegation that Jefferson fathered several of the children born to Sally Hemings, an attractive Monticello house slave. DNA tests conducted on family members in 1998 reinforced her assertions. More recently, scholars have uncovered disturbing evidence regarding Jefferson's justification for refusing to free his more than 600 slaves. In the latest expose, *Smithsonian Magazine* quotes passages from the Farm Book and subsequent letters in Jefferson's hand that suggest greed as his underlying motive. Calculating a "four per cent per annum" credit on the birth of each black child, Monticello's architect posits that slavery, far more than crops or husbandry, will yield a steady source of income for his plantation. He goes on to describe how "the small ones, aged 10–12, must of course be whipped if necessary to get them to work."

These heretofore suppressed statements obviously undercut the spirit of the Declaration of Independence, and my Monticello tour guide makes no mention of their discovery. However, the tour ticket now includes a popular slavery walk of the plantation grounds. On a path down a slope along Mulberry Row, some twenty buildings once held slave families and the

Vegetable gardens at Monticello in April. Photo by author.

workshops where they toiled. Restoration and reconstruction of these outbuildings is ongoing.

I linger at Monticello in the warm afternoon sun, take a seat along a wooded trail to view the "perfect house in a perfect setting," and saunter through the manicured vegetable gardens a second time. Enormous sums of money are required to maintain this house and grounds, and dedicated staff members like Debbie Donley worry that these investments may not be sustainable as the climate gradually warms.

The consensus among climatologists is that global warming now accounts for spring's arrival some seven to ten days earlier on average than its appearance in 1950. Comparisons with records kept by earlier observers like Aldo Leopold and

Henry David Thoreau indicate a significant two-week advance for seventeen species of birds, intermediate changes for eighteen other species, and no difference in arrival dates for twenty others, according to ecologist Amy Seidl. She notes that "some species of birds respond to climate change because they are biologically capable of drifting toward earlier migration, responding to temperature as a trigger to move." Labeling these species "advancers," she posits that they have "the genetic capacity to alter their phenology" because they likely have experienced climate changing events in the past and have passed along this genetic advantage over countless generations. "We know from changes in species' ranges from other warming times in Earth's history that they are more likely to undergo a change in distribution, becoming more common at the edge of their range or at higher elevations within it." Although such flexibility may allow "advancers" to respond to the changes in climate we are now experiencing, not all of these species possess the plastic response necessary to adapt to "simultaneous changes in prey or food availability." Species that time their reappearance to take advantage of peak food sources will remain especially vulnerable—whether these be insect pollinators that depend on specific flowering plants, or bird species (like the phoebe or hummingbird) that coordinate nesting activities in synchrony with preferred insect prey. In the last ten years researchers have identified more and more examples of these trophic mismatches—"species out of sync, arriving in the once-correct location but at a time when expanded resources have already passed them by." The ultimate consequences of such missed opportunities remain difficult to predict, especially given the complex ecological relationships at outdoor museums like Monticello.

The Great Songbird Swamp

Sawmills, everywhere we go, are going full blast. . . .
The edges of the Great Dismal Swamp are now being lumbered—the great cypress trees of the interior
have all been cut in years past. . . . A dogwood is in
bloom beside the Swamp, and the water in the canal
is a deep chocolate color.

EDWIN WAY TEALE, JOURNAL OF *North with the Spring*

Unlike its charismatic Okefenokee cousin, North Carolina's
Great Dismal Swamp received little attention within the conservation community. As a result, when Edwin and Nellie arrived, its seemingly limitless supply of pine, Atlantic white
cedar, black gum, tupelo bald cypress, and sweet gum poplar
continued to be ravaged. My wife had grown up beside the
swamp in nearby Elizabeth City, and we had driven along its
dark eastern edge many times on our way to visit her family.
A narrow column of cypress trees along Highway 17 provides
a thin curtain, behind which drift shadows of boats navigat-
ing the Intracoastal Waterway. More than 140 miles of logging
roads penetrate the interior of this vast wetland, along with
the remnants of eighteen canals. Prior to 1800 the Dismal
Swamp Lumber Company shipped over 1 million shingles cut
from majestic old-growth cypress and white cedar. And along

its margins in 1947, the sound of sawmills still roared "full blast."

Only after the swamp's resources were squandered was this unique east coast ecosystem finally protected. In 1973 the Union Camp Corporation made available 49,000 acres to the Nature Conservancy, which then donated the tract to the federal government. Today the Great Dismal Swamp National Wildlife Refuge, established to protect and restore this distinctive wetland, encompasses over 112,000 acres and abuts North Carolina's Dismal Swamp State Park. Stripped of its big trees and devoid of the Spanish moss and alligators that give the Okefenokee its allure, the Great Dismal appears rather tame and "only sparsely inhabited," as my predecessor noted.

Our middle daughter, Anna, an employee with the U.S. Fish and Wildlife Service, has arranged to meet me at the refuge headquarters located along an out-of-the-way road on the western edge of the swamp. Here, she introduces me to Chris Lowie, Dismal Swamp Refuge manager, a short, compact, easygoing young man with a thin mustache and a delightful sense of humor. He lets us borrow a government canoe and directs us to the Lake Drummond boat ramp. "Restoring the swamp is proving frustrating," Chris tells us, "especially given the increase in hurricanes, fires, and droughts." A sizable stand of Atlantic white cedar was toppled by Hurricane Isabel in 2003, and a massive wildfire in 2011 consumed thousands of replanted cypress, cedar, and longleaf seedlings. I'm reminded again of William Jordan's insight—only through mistakes and miscalculations can we truly come to know a piece of land.

Along a dirt road paralleling Railroad Ditch, Anna spots a juvenile black bear scuttling across downed trees through the marsh. The swamp is home to the largest population of black bears in eastern Virginia, and the refuge now sponsors a three-day bear hunt at the conclusion of its fall deer hunting season. The refuge also caters to local fisherman by maintaining a boat ramp at the road's end to facilitate crappy fishing, a spring tradition on Lake Drummond. Edwin and Nellie chartered a boat to access Drummond, and we plan to retrace their route via kayak the next day. Their guide, Captain William Crockett, a talkative former timber man, insisted that the 3,000-acre shallow body of water at the center of the swamp resulted from "a great fire in prehistoric times, told of in Indian legends." Geologists now believe that in fact an intense conflagration did burn over a long period, leaving behind a great depression that gradually filled with water. As we slide our canoe into the chocolate brown choppy waters of the lake, dark clouds gather overhead, the wind picks up, and rain begins. Anna spots an eagle's nest along the shoreline, and a few moments later, a magnificent adult American bald eagle drops from its perch and sails across the sky. We peer into the dense cover of young trees along shore, where catbirds, cardinals, and flycatchers flit among the branches. Teale's observation—"the teeming wild-life we had expected was not there"—still rings true.

A rising southwest wind begins to kick up ever-larger waves across the 3-mile shallow lake. Within minutes the full fury of a spring deluge arrives. In response, we strain to reach the dock, soaked and shivering as the temperature continues to plummet. Finally, racing for the inside of the truck, Anna and I wait out the storm, our hands pressed against the dashboard heater. When the sun finally returns, we follow a short board-walk trail to a single 800-year-old cypress snag, struck by light-ning in the recent past. This sad remnant of an old-growth for-est serves as an emblem of human avarice. We also stop to visit the Underground Railroad Education Pavilion, which tells the story of runaway slaves who escaped to safety within the con-fines of the Dismal Swamp. Communities of Indian and Afri-can American men and women, referred to as maroons, from the French word for "to flee," settled in the swamp decades before the Civil War. Recent research suggests that as many as 50,000 individuals may have taken up residence in this remote and inaccessible hideaway. Here fugitives built cabins, hunted deer and wild turkeys, and likely farmed small plots of elevated land. As logging operations expanded in the swamp, these maroon colonies began an active trade network with the outside world. In exchange for goods, some of the resident runaways may even have assisted captive slaves who were brought to the swamp to process cedar shingles. Many of these workers are believed to have settled nearby at the conclusion of the war. They found employment digging canals, manufacturing shingles, and sharecropping along the swamp's edge.

That evening I pick up a brochure describing the development of the shad boat industry along the mid-Atlantic coast. George Washington Creef designed these round-bottomed and shallow-keeled sailing crafts in the 1870s. He began to experiment with boats that could navigate the mouths of North Carolina and Virginia rivers in pursuit of migrating shad and other anadromous fish. The boat he perfected used Atlantic white cedar planks for its bottom boards and keel, and cedar stumps, cut into 2-inch slices, to produce lightweight, sturdy ribs. The immediate popularity of this design dramatically increased tree-harvesting operations in the Dismal Swamp in the last quarter of the nineteenth century.

The next morning Anna and I set out to retrace Edwin and Nellie's boat route. We park beside the Dismal Swamp Canal and paddle south along the Intracoastal Waterway, the oldest man-made canal in America, begun in 1793. Walls of vegetation block our view to the interior, while boats of various sizes chug past. "No Trespassing" signs hang from makeshift docks, a reminder that land abutting the waterway and purchased before 1973 remains in private hands. Twenty minutes in, we locate Feeder Ditch, with its "solidly massed banks of honeysuckle." Another plant species, invasive kudzu, has overtaken the honeysuckle and blanketed neighboring trees. Introduced to the United States by Japan in 1876, kudzu captured the imagination of American gardeners and became a favorite ornamental plant. Civilian Conservation Corps workers planted thousands of acres in kudzu during the Great Depression, and Teale lists this exotic as one of the "plants with strange names" introduced in an effort to restore the Ducktown desert. Known as a "miracle vine" during the 1940s, kudzu was seeded along southern roadways to help prevent soil erosion. However, with no natural competitors, the vines took over everything—trees, fences, power lines—sometimes growing as fast as 60 feet a year. Because kudzu resists traditional herbicides, it remains a significant environmental challenge for foresters and wildlife officials throughout the South.

Edwin photographed dozens of turtles, "flat, black, and as large as dinner plates," that plopped into the water on either side of Feeder Ditch. We paddle past painted turtles, stinkpots, ridge-backed snappers, and even an eastern box turtle that struggles to swim the channel. Several ribbon-thin water snakes thread their way ahead of us. My predecessor also described "a fleeting glimpse of one of those gold-and-blue birds of the Okefenokee, a prothonotary warbler," and I'm determined to show Anna one. We catch a faint glimpse of the warbler on several occasions, and then as we stop to watch another turtle, a male prothonotary wings above us and lands high up in a shrub. Its orange-gold head and blue-gray wings catch and hold the sun.

Mounds of brown scud collect along the bank beside water control structures that regulate the depth of the intracoastal canal. Anna stops to fish beside one of these, and I tell her the story of a young Robert Frost. Devastated when his love, Elinor, refused his proposal of marriage, Frost traveled to the Dismal Swamp intent on abandoning himself to its interior. He later claimed that he wandered for hours and survived through the luck of passing hunters. According to Chris Lowie, even now search parties are organized every few years to locate an individual who has wandered off-trail.

We eventually reach the small island at the head of Feeder Ditch where Edwin and Nellie disembarked in preparation for

"Captain" Crockett maneuvers his boat on Feeder Ditch. Photo by E. W. Teale. Edwin Way Teale Papers, Archives and Special Collections at the Thomas J. Dodd Research Center, University of Connecticut Libraries. Used with permission.

their ride around Lake Drummond. Here, a series of gates, operated electronically by the Army Corps of Engineers, raise and lower water levels between canal and lake. Three families have pitched tents on this tiny island, and I chat with one of the fathers. "We make this weekend outing to Drummond every spring," he tells me. "Living up in Chesapeake, it's the only way our kids can experience a sky full of stars." Bisecting the island is a set of railroad ties, part of the "narrow-gauge track" Captain Crockett utilized to haul his motorboat up to Lake Drummond. The "hand-operated wheel" Teale described has

The same "narrow gauge track" at Feeder Ditch in 2012. Photo by author.

been replaced by an electronic winch; otherwise, this mechanism still serves as the only method of boat transport. I study the tracks and peer into dust-covered windows of the same outbuilding my predecessor photographed.

As we retrace our route, drifting with the current, Anna outlines the future vision of the U.S. Fish and Wildlife refuge system. Their new model calls for sites like the Great Dismal Swamp, where no seriously endangered species remain, to offer greater visitor access—welcoming birdwatchers, adding historical signage, and reaching out to private landowners to expand refuge boundaries. The nearby Dismal Swamp State Park, with its modern two-story visitor center beside the highway, its numerous parking lots and extensive signage, its daily rental of canoes, kayaks, and bicycles, might serve as a model as well as a future partner. The refuge, she believes, might also expand its educational programming specifically designed to showcase Lake Drummond, especially now that the water body has been included in Virginia's elementary school curriculum. Getting schoolchildren in boats to tour the lake and experience the effects of resource extraction firsthand might help educate a new generation, one that remains too little informed about natural history and the federal government's role in preservation. Building a series of boardwalks modeled after Audubon's Corkscrew Swamp Sanctuary might also improve access for those interested in identifying some of the 200 avian species that feed or nest in this "Great Songbird Swamp."

As we prepare to return to the truck, a kingfisher launches from the bank, rattles across the canal, and bobs from its perch on the opposite shore. These blue-crested water birds are one of Anna's favorites. Their odd teetering behavior intrigued Teale, and he included various explanations for the "mystery of the tip-ups" in his chapter on the Dismal Swamp. One ornithologist theorized that the motion might allow water birds to communicate with one another above the sound of a rushing stream, while another hypothesized that the bobbing movements might mask their presence along the water's edge. Scientists have continued to investigate, and several promising theories have been put forth. My choice is a proposal by Lee Casperson that relies on both direct observation and mathematical modeling. In 1999 he theorized that the vertical bobbing motion in birds associated with streams, lakes, and the seashore "may aid a bird in acquiring visual information" as it peers through "the interference and distortion caused by reflection and refraction at the air/water boundary."

Teale ended his chapter with "an almost eerie sight," the death of thousands of honeybees blown off-course into the lake in their attempt to swarm. Detailed depictions of natural phenomena in the Great Dismal Swamp and in other wild sites like the New Jersey Pine Barrens, Outer Cape Cod, and Walden

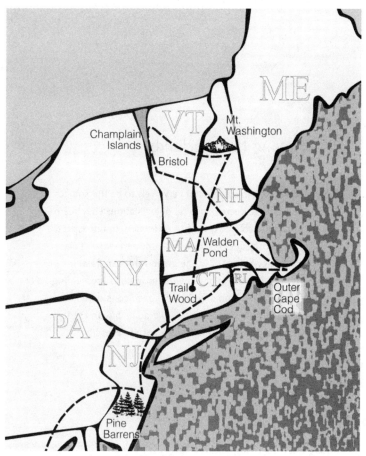

Detail of New Jersey and New England travels.

Pond attracted a readership numbering in the thousands. The copy of *North with the Spring* that I own, published in 1966, represents its nineteenth printing. Although it's impossible to gauge with precision the influence this volume has had on the environmental community, all of the sites listed above were vulnerable to development when Teale studied them. Each of these special places has since been preserved and protected for future generations to enjoy.

Saving the Pinelands

The Pine Barrens are not very likely to be the subject
of dramatic decrees or acts of legislation. They seem
to be headed slowly toward extinction. In retrospect,
people may one day look back upon the final stages
of the development of the great unbroken Eastern
city and be able to say at what moment all remaining
undeveloped land should have been considered no
longer a potential asset to individuals but an asset
to society at large—perhaps a social necessity.

JOHN McPHEE, *The Pine Barrens*

The Teales quickened their pace after leaving Virginia and entering the "more familiar surroundings" of the North. Edwin's
journal entries became more compact, as he began to rely more
on notes he had collected during earlier travels to many of
these same locations. There also was the complication of early
spring giving way to its later manifestations, for as the author
acknowledged, "in traveling north we could not and never attempted to keep up with the initial wave." Finally, their return
required them to face once more the palpable reminders of
their son's death. A sign at Fort Dix brought back a "wave of
bitter sadness—here it was that David was stationed on his
last Christmas in this country."

Ten weeks into my journey I arrive at the New Jersey Pine Barrens. I've been looking forward to this geographic anomaly—the largest surviving open space on the Eastern Seaboard between the northern forests of Maine and the Everglades—especially because I've driven close to its western border on countless occasions without ever stopping. In addition, as my mentor noted, "spring comes with especial beauty" to austere locations like "barrens or dunes or tarns." This scrubby pine forest had attracted little notoriety in 1947, and it wasn't until the 1960s that suburban development began to make incursions. Its uniqueness and these impending threats motivated journalist John McPhee to spent two years traveling deserted sand roads and befriending local inhabitants, who called themselves "pineys." According to McPhee, after a generation or two of isolation, "the pineys began to fear people from the outside, and travelers often reported that when they approached a cabin in the pines the people scattered and hid behind trees." In *The Pine Barrens*, he recounts the stories these inhabitants told and reports on the region's history of repeated industrial failures, unscrupulous land developers, and generations of immigrants who eked out a living by hunting, fishing, and growing fruits and vegetables in nutrient-starved sandy soil.

I begin my exploration of the pinelands at Batsto, a historic village in the southernmost corner of the barrens. Founded in 1766 by Charles Read, a noted ironmaster before the Revolutionary War, Batsto became renowned for bog iron beneath its surface, and as a result from 1773 to 1848 the furnace town expanded to include a post office, sawmill and gristmill, a horse stable, and a mansion built by William Richards. All of these structures have been restored, and I walk across fields carpeted in dandelions and framed in flowering dogwoods to reach the four-story house in the town center. Here a pile of nondescript whitish-gray rocks illustrates the low-grade metallic ore that put these barrens on the map. More impervious to rust than other iron, this "bog" variety nonetheless fell out of favor by

Historic mansion in Batsto Village. Photo by author.

the 1840s when high-grade bituminous coal and nearby iron deposits were discovered in western Pennsylvania. Over the next half-century ironworkers followed jobs west, and as a result, businesses failed and towns began to vanish back into the woods.

In 1876 Philadelphia industrialist Joseph Wharton purchased the entire town of Batsto. His ingenious plan called for damming up its local streams, flooding his holdings, connecting multiple reservoirs via canals, and selling the impounded water to Camden and Philadelphia. The grand scheme never materialized, however, and so Wharton expanded his agricultural operations at Batsto, cultivating cranberries and blueberries and developing a "gentleman's farm." The state of New Jersey purchased the Wharton holdings in 1954, and today these parcels form the core of Wharton State Forest. Over the years the state has restored the water-powered sawmill, which cuts white cedar shingles, and the gristmill, which grinds and sells local corn. I explore both of these industrial sites, and although neither of the mills is operating, I watch a pair of phoebes flit in and out of nearby sheds. I also visit the on-site naturalist, a talkative young man with thick-rimmed glasses and closely cropped dark hair. He tells me he grew up nearby and that he's delighted to have found a job so close to home. The list he keeps of spring phenology includes herring migrating up a local stream, the trailing arbutus blooming two weeks ahead of schedule, and early reports of pine warblers and purple martins. Great crested flycatchers and northern orioles are due any day, he tells me. His bird count from 2011 includes fifty-five bluebirds, seventy-seven tree swallows, and thirty-eight wrens in Batsto village alone by the end of May.

Fire and water together are responsible for the unique features of the Pine Barrens, according to John McPhee. Rainwater percolates rapidly through the sandy soil, and as a result, a reservoir equivalent in volume to "a lake seventy-five feet deep with a surface of a thousand square miles" lies beneath the forest. Fire has been the other major component in this ecosystem, and more than 400 blazes are reported annually. This high frequency of fire accounts for a uniform forest of pine. Ecologists point out that if fire were suppressed in the barrens, the typical pattern of forest succession would result in oaks, hickories, and red maples. However, wildfires have "generally stopped the march of natural succession" as woods repeatedly burn over and resprout. These wildfires sometimes rage out of control for weeks: in 1963 a massive conflagration scorched 200,000 acres around Chatsworth, destroying 450 structures and claiming seven lives.

The entire barrens, not just historic Batsto, display an odd mix of grandeur and depravity. The people who live here surrounded by woods have been stigmatized for generations as hostile, ill-bred, and lazy, although the author of *The Pine Barrens* found them "tolerant, with an attractive spirit of live and let live." Most of the pineys McPhee met were hardworking and shy. After they got to know him, they "generously share[d] their tables, which often include[d] new-potato stews and cranberry potpies."

Driving down arrow-straight, two-lane roads, hemmed in on either side by stunted pines, I suddenly come upon fields of blueberries, white in blossom as far as I can see. In other lowland openings where water pools, workers have fashioned cranberry bogs whose walled-in paddocks and earthen dikes remind me of South Carolina rice plantations. As I walk and bird along my drive to Chatsworth, the largest and most progressive town in the center of the pinelands, I notice robins, cardinals, goldfinches, tree swallows, bluebirds, pine warblers, and even an osprey. The village itself, anchored by a fire station and an eclectic grocery store, features neatly trimmed single-story residences, many sporting a fresh coat of paint, along a network of intersecting streets. Chatsworth reminds me of towns in Suffolk County, Long Island, except for the realization that here a visit to the neighboring village in any direction requires a 20-mile drive through desolate woods.

The stories McPhee uncovered about unsolved murders, airplane crashes, an Italian prince, and the Jersey Devil all seem plausible as I peer down the rutted tracks on the outskirts of Chatsworth. Edwin and Nellie spent time sauntering these same wood roads, "where our footfalls were muffled in the fine sand" and where a breeze through pine needles "sang one of the oldest songs on earth." This scenery brought back earlier images for Edwin: carpenter bees and sphagnum frogs recalled the Okefenokee, and a bluebird, "alighting on the rough bark of a pitch pine," brought to mind an early moment along the Tamiami.

Teale's brief chapter on the Pine Barrens includes many details about rare insects entomologists had collected in this sandy bog. He recounts the discovery of the Hessel's hair-streak, the "first new butterfly discovered in the northeastern United States in forty years." These rare butterflies still inhabit the Jersey Barrens, although I was not fortunate enough to see one. Their major threat today is from deer that browse on the white cedar saplings where the insects lay their eggs. New Jersey's deer population has increased exponentially since Teale visited. Deer herds are responsible for damaging ornamental plantings and agricultural crops and for causing hundreds of automobile collisions in the barrens. In a controversial move, the Fish and Wildlife Service recently sponsored a community-based deer management program that included professional hunters who disposed of hundreds of adult deer that had been baited with corn kernels scattered around neighborhood parks. During the 2012 season, hunters killed 50,000 white-tailed deer across the state.

A changing climate has introduced other new threats to the Pine Barrens. The southern pine bark beetle, which tradition-ally had been killed by subzero temperatures, has moved into New Jersey and begun to ravage large swaths of susceptible co-nifers. Legislation aimed at thinning the forest and conducting controlled burns, strategies that have reduced beetle numbers in southern states, was vetoed in New Jersey in 2012. In other political action, the governor lobbied for a proposed 22-mile natural gas pipeline that would cut a scar across the barrens. Environmentalists strenuously objected, and the Pinelands Commission, an independent state and federal agency tasked with jurisdiction over this National Reserve, deadlocked 7–7, which means that the pipeline will not be built—at least for now.

Teale concludes his portrait of these pinelands focused on an "ancient song of spring"—the lone call of a whippoorwill. I heard this bird's plaintive note only once on my excursion— along a quiet moonlit street on Fripp Island. These once-com-mon nightjars are now rare in the Northeast, having declined by 57 percent over the past forty years, according to the National Audubon Society. Crepuscular in habit, whippoorwills require an open understory beneath deciduous trees in order to lay their eggs and hunt for insects. Ornithologists have been able to determine that female whippoorwills are sensitive to the lunar cycle: they lay their clutch of eggs to hatch some ten days before a full moon. In this way adult birds can forage all night in bright moonlight to capture the large quantities of moths and other insects that their nestlings need. Encroaching suburban development, fire suppression, and a decline in insect numbers are likely responsible for the whippoorwill's decline.

As the opening quote indicates, the author of *The Pine Barrens* was not optimistic that this unique parcel would be saved. Competing proposals in the 1960s pitted massive development projects against calls for land protection. The most elaborate of these plans envisioned a supersonic jetport, "four times as large as Newark Airport, LaGuardia, and Kennedy put together," as well as the development of a new 250,000-person city. McPhee toured the proposed site with Herbert Smith, its principal architect, who described his plan as "a happy marriage between conservation and economic development." A group of pineland conservationists put forth a different vision, one that emphasized stewardship of this undeveloped refuge and called for conservation of all 90,000 acres. Although John McPhee remained skeptical, his best-selling volume generated an immediate and effective public outcry for preservation. Ultimately these voices proved decisive, and in November 1978 the National Parks and Recreation Act established the country's first national reserve, a public-private partnership with a management plan designed to promote the orderly development of the Pine Barrens "so as to preserve and protect the significant and unique natural, ecological, agricultural, archaeological, historical, scenic, cultural, and recreational resources." The Pinelands National Reserve, which today includes 1.1

million acres of farms, forests, and wetlands, serves as a dramatic illustration of how committed local residents working in partnership with conservation organizations have been able to persuade elected officials to protect vulnerable wild lands. The preservation of these barrens also demonstrates the power of a talented individual with a compelling narrative to share.

⁄ ⁄ ⁄

I cancel my reservation at Wharton State Forest as the temperature plummets and a driving rain begins. The next six hours are a blur of highway miles. When I reach my New Hampshire home, a young woman named Andrea, whom my wife has taken in as a tenant during my absence, greets me at the door. Exhausted from the long drive, I push into the kitchen and pull up a chair. As I begin asking her questions, Andrea seems nervous, reticent, unsure how to respond. Only when I mention my last name does she relax, welcoming one whom until that moment she had judged an intruder.

"Susie's gone to dinner at the neighbors. And she didn't mention you were coming home."

I spend the night with my wife in a bed I've not occupied for seventy-five days. The three-note "cheer-cheer-cheer" of the male cardinal wakes me, and the "ok-a-lee" of the red-winged blackbird and the twitter of tree swallows confirm that I am home. Our phoebe, reminiscent of Jefferson's phoebe, flits back and forth to her moss-lined nest. My favorite pair, the bluebirds, whose modesty was the subject of Native American legends and whose numbers were in decline during Teale's trip, sit atop the nest box, standing sentinel to ward off swallows. The loss of natural tree cavities and open field habitat, coupled with competition from introduced species like the starling and the house sparrow, reduced bluebird numbers. Lovers of these birds responded, however, urging community groups like the Boy Scouts to construct nest boxes and sponsor bluebird trails. These artificial cavities proved effective, and eastern bluebird numbers have increased by 2.4 percent per year for each year since 1966.

Susie and I go fishing on the Connecticut River the next morning. Here a muskrat glides toward shore with a mouthful of grass, a belted kingfisher rattles overhead, and a great blue heron, perhaps the same bird I watched along the Anhinga Trail, stands motionless against the bank. The half-submerged shape of a floating log triggers my attention, and later, as we secure the kayaks to the roof, an adult bald eagle glides down the center of the river. Eagles were a rare sight when we arrived in 1985. Now, almost three decades later, they have become quite common. A year ago an eagle pair established a nest in a tall pine on a nearby farm, and Charles Broley, Rachel Carson, and Edwin Teale would all be pleased to know that the population of breeding eagles in New Hampshire has increased from less than ten to more than eighty birds in the past twenty-five years.

Another common raptor, the turkey vulture, was virtually unknown across New England in 1947. The species began to migrate north after World War II, following a trail of roadkill along Eisenhower administration federal highways. Their hunched silhouettes and dark tilting shadows were near constant companions on my trip. Black vultures, their close cousins, still prefer the warmth of southern climes. Hundreds of black vultures had roosted along the Suwannee River, and one desperate individual, apparently snatched from its perch, flapped wildly as its underwater adversary pulled tail, torso, and finally hideous head below.

Over the next few days I search in vain for flowering bloodroot and yellow trout lilies in the back pasture and listen for the bell-clear note of the northern oriole. A neotropical migrant, orioles leave their wintering grounds in Central America in late February and follow the season northward as food emerges. Teale recorded his first Baltimore oriole in Glasgow, Virginia, on May 11, and I spotted one of these brilliant songsters at

Monticello on April 19. According to my seasonal records, between 1986 and 2011 the first oriole almost always arrived in Westmoreland during the first week of May. We usually see the male hopping among blossoms on the flowering quince and calling from the crown of a nearby red maple. This spring, due to record warming, the quince has already exploded in red weeks ahead of schedule, and yet neither of its primary nectar feeders, the oriole or the ruby-throated hummingbird, has arrived.

On May 6 six individuals show up to pick fiddlehead ferns along a low-lying bank on the Connecticut River. These itinerants form yet another migratory wave in spring's northward progress. The trilling of toads, "the most beautiful of all our batrachian sounds," according to my predecessor, soon fills the evening air. Toads once gathered in large numbers at our backyard pond before I foolishly added half a dozen wood frogs, enamored by their ducklike quacking, together with a couple of snapping turtles I pulled off the road. Miscalculations like these, as well as successful reintroductions and plantings, account for the intimacy Susie and I now feel for our 10-acre homestead. As my friend John Elder recognized, we choose our place, and then over time the place chooses us.

As daytime temperatures approach 70 degrees, I get an urge to turn over the garden. The rich smell of broken loam calls to mind my father and his seasonal ritual of mounding up soil, casting out stones, and kneeling to drop in seeds. For him, giving up gardening had been even more difficult than relinquishing his car keys. In his last two years, we drove to the Pennsylvania farm mostly to sit on the porch, listen for birds, and retell stories of earlier harvests. His fondest hope had been that this place would serve as a family gathering spot, a retreat for tensions to ease. That dream never quite materialized, however.

Author Bill McKibben received an honorary degree at the university where I teach in 2012, and I met with Bill after his commencement address. He was delighted to learn of my re-tracing, calling *North with the Spring* one of his favorite books. "It's an accurate portrayal of a single season, and therefore something we can turn to in this age of climate instability." The next morning, with six states yet to experience, I set off west across Massachusetts for Woodchuck Lodge, the summer retreat of John Burroughs, America's most popular natural history writer in the generation before Teale. Edwin had planned his own pilgrimage to honor Burroughs and had arrived at the writer's Riverby home along the Hudson on the very night that it burned to the ground. With newfound stoicism, he concluded his entry for the evening of June 5 with this sentence: "How strange a thing that, in time and space, our journey of four months and fourteen-thousand miles should have brought us to Riverby at the precise hour of its tragic end."

Teale maintained an abiding affection for John Burroughs, in part because the older writer provided a model for introducing backyard nature in a genial tone and because he, too, was deeply nostalgic for lost boyhood days. Burroughs chose to be buried in a simple grave plot on a hillside above Woodchuck Lodge in sight of the Catskill Mountains. Teale planned a pilgrimage to this site the year following his spring excursion, and he included his impressions in an addendum to his journal. Looking out from Burroughs' gravesite, he noted "the quilted mountainside fields beyond—fields that seemed held together by the embroidery of stone walls."

When I arrive at Burroughs' ancestral farm in Roxbury, New York, the rustic two-story house, constructed by his brother Curtis, remains just as it was when the famous man occupied it. The parlor, sitting room, kitchen, and tiny bedroom all appear like appendages to a wide front porch, where Burroughs frequently sat to write. Indigo buntings are singing in the treetops, and I listen for the call of the ovenbird, with its distinctive "teacher, teacher" cadence that Burroughs first described and Teale later recorded on his trip to Riverby. A woodchuck scurries across a path that leads up to the grave. The old man once boasted that he shot eighty of these pasture marmots during a single season.

The "quilted mountainside fields" Edwin marveled at have returned to forest all over New England, thanks in large part to consolidation in the dairy industry. In 1933 the county in which Roxbury lies was the nation's third largest dairy producer; today Delaware County, New York, ranks 210th nationally in terms of milk production. Wildlife has benefited from this abandonment, but the human cost has been enormous. Thousands of families were forced to accept factory wages and relocate to metropolitan areas to the east. Many of these who loved their lost farms became the devoted readers of Edwin Way Teale. In the meantime, rural Massachusetts, Vermont, and New Hampshire, as well as Upstate New York, witnessed the return of wild creatures like the coyote, fox, bobcat, beaver, fisher, pine marten, porcupine, and the black bear, whose arrival on Cape Cod was imminent.

The Stuff of Legend

Questions abound amid the swirl of reports surrounding the black bear that crossed the canal last
week and blazed a trail eastward toward the Outer
Cape. It's the first time a bear has been documented
on Cape Cod, home to furry mammals of less
impressive stature, since colonial times, wildlife officials say. Several unconfirmed sightings over the last
few days indicate the bear may have crossed through
Wellfleet and into Truro.

KAIMI ROSE LUM, "BEAR BUZZ HITS OUTER CAPE"

Susie and I, with our neighborhood friends John and Robin
Stronk, cross the Bourne Bridge on June 8, the same day on
which Edwin and Nellie battled a nor'easter as they arrived on
the Cape. We head directly for Race Point Beach, excited to
spend a day along the Atlantic coast in bright, warm sunshine.
The parking lot is already half-full, and we quickly pull off our
shoes and head for the water's edge. The ocean is frigid, and the
sea air tastes strongly of salt. We walk north for several miles
along the Great Beach, coined as such by Henry David Thoreau
and later commemorated by Henry Beston in his classic work,
The Outermost House. "A great ocean beach runs north and
south unbroken, mile lengthening into mile," Beston had written, calling these sands "the end or the beginning of the world."

This most storied stretch of coastline anywhere in the East was deemed "wild and rank" by Thoreau, who walked its entire length on two occasions in the 1850s. The feel of wet sand underfoot, along with toe-cramping chill, brings back memories of Boneyard Beach and Fripp Island from two months earlier.

Heavy spring showers had curtailed Teale's progress along the length of Cape Cod in June. A powerful nor'easter lashed the island for two days, preventing the couple from walking the beach and forcing them instead to make repeated visits to the sand dunes, a topography rich in childhood associations. Sand hills, with their "mystery of the far-away," brought back memories of that golden period of exploration and freedom on his grandparents' farm near the southeastern tip of Lake Michigan. Although the farm had vanished—the property was sold when the house burned to the ground—its significance continued to haunt the author, who sought out topography sculpted by wind and sand whenever possible. The "Lilliputian flora" crowning the headlands along Cahoon's Hollow and Pamet Point have changed little since Teale's day, and where we park sits an identical "gem of a small pond, its surface dotted with buds of yellow water lilies." Looking out from these headlands, which reminded Thoreau of the crow's nest of a ship, we spot a dozen eiders riding the surf and further out, large dark shapes bobbing in the waves.

These are "horseheads," male gray seals that together with their smaller female counterparts watch us as we work our way down from the bluff. These sleek mammals possess the same intelligent eyes we have noticed in our neighbor's border collie. Teale makes no mention of seals in his journal, for almost every species of these Atlantic pinnipeds had been extirpated south of the Canadian Maritimes by the time he visited. A bounty of five dollars per nose, imposed by fisherman who stubbornly blamed seals for depleting codfish stocks, led to this dramatic decline. Teale's contemporary John Hay, another in the long line of Cape Cod naturalists, expressed great pleasure when he saw "two harbor seals of good size, swimming twenty or thirty feet outside the beach." He confided that these "intelligent and appealing animals" had "suffered great persecution," and as a result were "much less numerous in Cape waters than they used to be." It was not until passage of the Marine Mammal Protection Act of 1972 that seal numbers gradually began to rebound. Today, it is estimated that more than 15,000 gray seals feed in the waters off Cape Cod, and their proliferation has sparked a new controversy, for many residents hold them responsible for the growing number of great white sharks that patrol offshore. Robert Finch, our guide the following day, once put himself between a herd of sixty northern harbor seals and the nearby ocean at Jeremy Point. He described the encounter as something between "a school of dolphins and a pack of large dogs" until he reached down to touch a seal moving beside him. At that moment, "the animal opened its mouth, snarling and snorting, barking and feinting at me with sharp canine teeth."

We settle into a house on a quiet street in Wellfleet within walking distance of Village Pond, the site where sixteen men, Miles Standish and William Bradford among them, camped on their second night after landing on American soil in November 1620. I can feel the layered depth of the place the next morning when I stand beside the pond and look out across to a forested island. Images of Fort Sumter, the tabby ruins on Bulls Island, and a solitary bison at Payne's Prairie come to mind. I also remember a near sleepless night spent in a nearby cemetery during high school when a spur-of-the-moment road trip with four friends failed to locate a cheap motel. Decades later, Susie and I pitched our tent in Truro and spent a glorious week hiking and biking on National Seashore trails with our girls.

Later, we rent bicycles and ride from Wellfleet to Orleans along the famed Cape Cod Rail Trail. This paved path follows the old rail bed that once connected Boston to Provincetown, carrying tourists to the end of the Cape and fish to a hungry city as early as 1873. Trains continued to haul freight along this line until the mid-1960s, after which tracks were torn up and a bike path installed. Along the way, we notice dozens of red-winged blackbirds and several pairs of osprey hovering over freshwater ponds. At a crowded creamery where we stop for ice cream I watch a phoebe bringing food to her four fidgety nestlings. The bike path bisects Nickerson State Park, a place wild enough to include fox scat, turkey tracks, deer pellets, as well as the songs of chestnut-sided, magnolia, and yellow-rumped warblers.

We peddle through the town of Eastham, made famous by Henry Beston, whose *Outermost House* had already gone through half a dozen printings by 1947. I'd been perplexed by the absence of Beston's name in Teale's chapter on Cape Cod. Later, I found this unpublished entry describing a 1948 meeting between the pair: "He came in a big, rawboned man with a square face, in a checkered sport jacket. While I was attracted to many aspects of Beston, there was no simplicity on which we could rest at ease. . . . He was swollen with 'ideas too big to be expressed,' and everything was inflated, blown up, until I longed for a pin. . . . He has his good points, but one of them is not simplicity. I longed for clear spring water such as I find in the simple, sincere people I know."

One of these "simple, sincere people" Teale relied on was Rachel Carson, who admired Henry Beston and learned from his vivid depictions. She credits his sonorous poetic descriptions of ocean life with helping her develop her own literary voice. "Behind me, in my footprints," Beston had written, "luminous patches burned. With the double-ebb moonlight and tide, the deepening brims of the pools took shape in smoldering, wet fire." He went on to explain the science of phosphorescence: how bacteria had invaded the sand fleas' tissues, infecting and ultimately killing the creatures. In his walks along the Great Beach, he often stopped to study their "huge porcelain eyes and water-grey body one core of living fire."

The following morning we drive to Provincetown, where Edwin and Nellie had stopped for "lobster lunch at the Bonnie Doone" and where Bill Bryson lamented that he had seldom seen a place "so singularly devoted to sucking money out of tourists." With Bryson in mind, we avoid the downtown and choose instead to walk out across a stone jetty that offers access to Long Point Beach. Fishermen settled here in 1818 and erected a lighthouse in 1826. Thoreau visited the village of Long Point, reporting that lobsters were plentiful in town. He also commented on the "dreary peep of the piping plover," a sound that "most perfectly revives the impression which the beach has made." Like egrets and ibises, Atlantic piping plovers were decimated by hunters for the millinery trade prior to 1900. The population rebounded and then experienced a second decline at midcentury due to pressure from ocean front development, increased recreation, and beach stabilization projects. Edwin fails to mention the piping plover among his "List of Birds Seen" during his trip north. Today, much of Long Point's sandy expanse is cordoned off to protect nesting plovers, beautiful little wading birds we are able to identify by their black collars and bright orange legs. Placed on the endangered species list in 1986, piping plover numbers have increased on Cape Cod from 18 pairs in 1985 to 82 pairs recorded in the summer of 2011. Although over 200 chicks hatched that year, only 90 survived to fledge. Late spring storms wash away their scrapes, the nests that plovers build directly on the sand, and crows, coyotes, skunks, and foxes all prey on exposed chicks. Fish and Wildlife officials are experimenting with devices called "exclosures," cages built over the nest designed to keep out predators and allow adult birds to enter. They also have contemplated poisoning crows, believed to be responsible for one-third of plover egg losses each year.

We tour the Highland Lighthouse in North Truro that afternoon. Thoreau once stayed with the keeper in this solitary ocean house and commented on the reflective lamp positioned only feet away from where he slept. "I thought as I lay there, half-awake and half-asleep . . . how many sleepless eyes from far out on the ocean stream—mariners of all nations spinning their yarns through the various watches of the night—were directed toward my couch." Edwin and Nellie stopped at the Highland Light on their first day just as "great rollers [were] piling on the shore." The force of these waves gradually undercut the sand foundation so severely that by 1990 the lighthouse stood within 100 feet of the water's edge. In response, in 1996 at a cost of $1,650,000, the 404-ton structure was lifted with hydraulic jacks, mounted on rollers, set on rails, and moved back 450 feet from its original location. We tour the light and learn the story of the nearby Jenny Lind Tower, which was moved piece by piece from Boston to North Truro in 1927 by a wealthy attorney who idealized the singer.

On his final day, as the storm abated, Edwin positioned himself beside a headland dune where he observed the activities of a resident ant colony. His detailed account of their foraging behavior, which occupies three full pages in *North with the Spring*, illustrates one of the few places where the author simply copied his journal entry. On our final day, John Stronk and I have arranged to tour the Wellfleet kettle ponds in the heart of Cape Cod National Seashore. Signed into law by the Kennedy administration in 1961, this federal designation saved 43,500 acres of the Outer Cape from the onslaught of residential development that had already ravaged much of the lower half. The legislation was unique because, for the first time, the government created a preserve out of land held primarily in private hands. There are still more than 600 inholdings, some with long-term leases and others that will never become available to the government. Public-private partnerships like this, and the more recent New Jersey Pine Barrens, illustrate the creativity now required to preserve vulnerable wild lands.

Acclaimed author Robert Finch begins our tour by pointing out a stand of black gum trees, called "beetlebungs" by early residents of Martha's Vineyard. The wood was used to make the mallet head, or beetle, needed to drive bungs, wooden corks, into casks and barrels. Next, he explains the formation of the numerous ponds we walk around—Gull, Higgins, Williams, Horseleech, Slough, and Herring—how massive chunks of glacial ice buried by till slowly melted, leaving behind these deep freshwater ponds. Here, men cut ice in Thoreau's day, and alewives still spawn, after following the contours of the narrow Herring River from the ocean inland. We saunter past numerous private residences, including the house of the loquacious oysterman whom Thoreau also stayed with in his travels. The home, with its "great number of windows at one end," according to the Concord sage, appears well kept with a fresh coat of paint and new cedar shingles. Bob quotes from memory several of the comments Thoreau penned about the odd oysterman and his even more peculiar family.

A number of the houses we pass exemplify the flat-roofed "modern" Bauhaus architectural style of Walter Gropius, who occupied one of these homes in the 1950s. Bob tells us that the National Park Service had to be persuaded to save several of these structures when their leases expired, and they became government property. We debate the merits of setting aside these homes to be used as affordable alternatives for town employees—firemen and policemen—and for the dwindling stock of fisherman, the backbone of the Cape's economy for generations. Bob also points out modest summer cottages and former hunting camps, now owned by wealthy urbanites who still prefer a rustic, unembellished experience, even as they now entertain their grandchildren.

Foxes, turkeys, deer, opossums, coyotes, fishers, and even pine martens have all been documented within National Seashore boundaries since 1960. And now, for the first time in the recorded history of the Cape, this list includes a black bear. As a *USA Today* headline earlier in the week announced: "The biggest sensation on Cape Cod right now isn't the lobster, the

A young black bear, the first of its kind in two hundred years, visits Cape Cod. Permission by John Stronk.

historic lighthouses, or its rolling sand dunes. It's not even a Kennedy. It's a bear."

As if on schedule, as we complete our long loop and load into cars, a beautiful, lustrous 200-pound black bear steps out onto the road and ambles along beside us. The bear seems unperturbed by our close presence, and I have an opportunity to study its rich dark fur, its chocolate-brown snout, and its muscular haunches as it strides beside us. We follow the bear's progress for several hundred yards before the animal turns north and scrabbles up a slope. It halts at the hill's crest to inspect a rotting pine snag, and with several effortless swipes, pulls away decaying bark. Over the next several minutes the bear divides its attention between the rotting tree and our parked car. During that time, it rears up on its hind legs to inspect the snag more closely, and then settles back on its haunches with its snout turned in our direction. After another minute of indecision, this "most notorious visitor of the summer" moves slowly out of sight behind the ridge.

Bob Finch has driven off by the time the bear disappears, and so John and I debate what to do next—leave the animal to pursue its course, or intervene in an attempt to protect it. News reports have encouraged residents to alert a Fish and Wildlife emergency rescue team. We decide to make the call, imagining the risk the bear will face as it attempts to cross Route 6 that evening.

When Bob calls that evening, I tell him of our decision. He listens without comment and includes the story of the bear in his weekly public radio broadcast to listeners on the Cape. Reflecting on our remarkable luck that day, Bob suggests that our "impeccable environmental decision" to intervene somehow strikes him as wrong. In his view the bear had earned the right to complete its journey, and our interruption, while displaying the "sober, civilized virtues of caution, consideration, and conservation," had in fact cut short what might have been an "improbable, admirable accomplishment." The bear's pioneering sojourn might have become the stuff of legend, a heroic tale for children celebrating "curiosity, courage, exploration, and skill at evading discovery."

In fact, the bear was tranquilized, dropped from the tree it climbed, and transported off-island that evening. It woke up the next morning safe in mainland woods. John Stronk is convinced we did the right thing, and I remain ambivalent. The creature was unquestionably savvy, negotiating the length of the island without incident and plotting its safe return. However, the same might be said for an adventurous mountain lion that journeyed from South Dakota as far as Connecticut. It was hit and killed attempting to cross a highway late one night.

Several weeks later I read in the *Boston Globe* that the same bear, identified by its radio collar, had been "rescued" a second time—pulled from a tree in a Boston suburb. In a strange way, I feel gratified to learn that the bear remains restless, ever on the move. It lets me imagine the story's new ending, one in which our hero finds an equally adventurous mate, and together they return to the Outer Cape. Thanks to the efforts of conservationists and writers like Edwin Way Teale, John Hay, and Robert Finch, this federal preserve may someday be wild enough to support a family of black bears.

From Deep Cut to Sudbury Meadow

On average, plants in Concord appear to flower now
seven days earlier than they did when Thoreau made
his observations in 1852–1858. . . . Temperatures in
eastern Massachusetts have increased more rapidly
than in many other areas of the world due to the
combination of global warming and the urban heat
island effect.

ABRAHAM MILLER-RUSHING AND RICHARD PRIMACK, "GLOBAL
WARMING AND FLOWERING TIMES IN THOREAU'S CONCORD"

On June 11, 1851, Henry David Thoreau recorded "a beautiful summer night, not too warm, moon not quite full," as he
sauntered along the rail bed from Walden Pond to Fair Haven. When he ascended out of the Deep Cut, he could feel
"a warmed stratum of air, air that yet remembers the sunny
banks—of the laborer wiping his brow, of the bee humming
amid flowers. No one, to my knowledge, has observed the minute differences in the seasons. Hardly two nights are alike."
Edwin Teale so admired Thoreau that he fashioned a replica of
his Walden cabin at Trail Wood in Connecticut. He also paid
homage to the sage by spending almost twenty years observing
the minute differences in the seasons. As he looked out across
Walden Pond in June 1947, cataloguing insects and birds, he

felt a similar quickening of the spirit, noting that spring "still comes with the age-old beauty of wildflowers and the age-old song of woodland birds."

In his pilgrimage around Walden, Teale had sauntered alone while Nellie remained in the car. He hoped to absorb "the spirit and history of Concord's past," which for him offered "the greatest natural-human phenomenon in the country." Walking slowly, he noticed a "wasp chewing on a faded pasteboard legal notice," the sizzle of a cicada, "like a partially opened pop bottle," and the droppings from feeding caterpillars, falling like a "fine rain pattering on the foliage of the bushes." He also described the "pink and white bells of the blueberry bushes," bushes in blossom ahead of Thoreau's calendar, and already turned to firm, green fruit sixty-five years later when I arrive at Walden Pond on that same calendar date.

Now protected, a key component of the pond's preservation is constraint. The parking lot is gated, a fee is charged to access the site, and the trail encircling Walden includes strands of braided wire on either side. At every few yards along the path signs read, "Please Stay on Trail" and "Violators Subject to Fines." Although necessary to prevent further damage, such restraints somehow violate the spirit of Thoreau. I follow the trail toward Deep Cut, determined to retrace my predecessor's precise route along the Fitchburg line. Here, among the cinders, the "smell of engine grease" remains pungent. The flat, fertile fields below, once planted in asparagus, have now become a pumpkin patch. A train roars past toward Boston enveloping me in the same "smoke and tornado of wind" my predecessor experienced. In place of an Oldsmobile hubcap and a rusting highway bridge, I pass a Styrofoam cup, plastic banners, and illegible graffiti. The train station in Concord is boarded up, and the uniformed guard on the platform casts a wary eye. On my way back to the pond a second locomotive charges past, signaling my trespass with a loud long whistle. Rules regarding public access have changed since the events of September

Looking out across Walden Pond in June. Photo by author.

11, and I'm hardly surprised to see an Amtrak pickup trundle down the tracks just as I reach the pond.

Dozens of people are swimming, fishing, or walking the trail loop this morning. Oak trees lean out over the water, their lobed leaves reflecting a deep shade of green. Several northern orioles call across the pond, "singing the rich contralto notes" Teale had heard during his spring sojourn. He encountered only one other visitor that morning, a writer named Lloyd Graham, who had recently purchased a copy of the Modern Library edition of *Walden*, which Teale edited. Graham had trouble believing that his guide that morning was the author, who later wrote: "It always seems disillusioning to people!" He might have been wearing a tie, or it might have been his instinctive aloofness.

As a young man Thoreau had made a fire that ultimately consumed hundreds of acres of woods in nearby Fair Haven. Teale makes mention of this mishap in his journal, and then goes on to write: "He set greater woods on fire—a blaze Concordians, in the main, never comprehended." One of these ideas was the suggestion that every town maintain "a primitive forest, of five hundred or a thousand acres," and that all of Walden Woods should be protected. More than a century would pass before this recommendation was acted upon. In 1939 E. B. White penned an ironic essay directed at Thoreau: "I knew I must be nearing your woodland retreat when the Golden Pheasant lunchroom came into view—with Sealtest ice cream, toasted sandwiches, hot frankfurters, waffles, tonics and lunches." At the time Walden Woods included an amusement park and baseball field, and efforts to preserve the cabin site languished even after the author's reputation became firmly established. During the 1950s throngs of sightseers, sometimes numbering as many as 10,000 on a single summer day, descended on the place. To highlight this situation, the author of *North with the Spring* catalogued every scrap of trash he encountered along the trail. His list includes "one hundred and sixteen beer cans . . . the remains of 14 campfires . . . half-eaten sandwiches . . . comic books . . . firecrackers . . . a baby-food jar . . . the thumb of a leather glove . . . and a dollar bill." Teale continued to do what he could to promote Thoreau's name and protect his sacred grove. As president of the Thoreau Society in the 1960s, he marshaled support to prevent Boston bulldozers from "building imitation Coney Island beaches" at Walden Pond.

Ultimately, the Commonwealth of Massachusetts, which purchased the property, imposed a limit of 1,000 visitors per day to prevent further degradation. The fence I found confining represents one of many "crowd control measures" implemented to manage the 700,000 visitors who pay homage at Walden Pond each year. Development pressures continued to mount along the edges of the state reservation, however, and in response, Don Henley, a recording artist with the rock band the Eagles, donated funds and galvanized support to purchase a 60-acre buffer around the preserve. As a result, "the nobler animals that have been exterminated"—moose, deer, bear, turkey, and beaver—making Thoreau's life in nature "lamentably incomplete"—have returned to the woods where the famous writer roamed.

Thoreau's meticulous record keeping of seasonal change in Concord is proving to be as valuable as his literary masterpieces. As the chapter epigraph illustrates, ecologists now utilize his journals, along with records kept by Alfred Hosmer, a Concord shopkeeper and amateur botanist, to assess the effects of climate alteration. The mean annual temperature in Concord has increased 2.4 degrees Celsius in the past 150 years, according to Richard Primack, author of *Walden Warming*. "Highbush blueberry, a native shrub, and yellow wood sorrel, a native herb, are now flowering 21 and 32 days earlier than they did 150 years ago, respectively."

One of Primack's primary concerns is what he calls "phantom plants," species that Thoreau described which are now either missing from the Concord environs or extremely rare. He estimates that if nothing is done to prevent further losses, "around half of the species that Thoreau observed in Concord will no longer be present in a few decades . . . they are destined for local extinction." Along with other ecologists Primack has suggested a strategy called "assisted colonization" to protect wild plants threatened by warming temperatures. This plan involves moving seeds and plants to sites that feature cooler conditions or higher elevations, places like the Berkshire Mountains or areas of southern New Hampshire and Vermont that might approximate the seasons of Walden Pond many decades ago.

Primack and his graduate students have compared bird arrival dates as well as flowering times for numerous plants. His conclusions for avian data indicate that three species now arrive earlier; fifteen do not appear to have changed arrival dates; and four species—the indigo bunting, ovenbird, wood thrush, and bobolink—actually arrive later in spring than they did 100 years ago. Collating this information with mist net data collected by the Manomet Center for Conservation Science, he determined that the number of birds netted each year has decreased by one-third over the past three decades and that "average arrival dates for eight of the thirty-two species studied are getting earlier over time." In addition, the synchrony between plant flowering and bird arrival has been disrupted, and these changes "will be to the advantage of some species and disadvantage of others, although it is difficult to predict the winners and losers." Reiterating Amy Seidl's predictions, Primack concludes that potentially catastrophic consequences may result from severing dependencies among plants, insects, birds, and animals that have evolved together over thousands of years.

Walden Warming ends by sketching two potential scenarios for the pond in the future. In the first, Concord residents experience a climate like that of South Carolina in Thoreau's day, and as a result Walden Pond no longer freezes. Ski villages in the White Mountains have been abandoned, massive steel flood gates protect Boston Harbor, and the Outer Cape has been broken into a series of smaller islands. In an alternate view, "nations have recognized limits to growth and responded by implementing measures that substantially reduce the consumption of fossil fuels." In this scenario ice still forms on Walden Pond, and houses in downtown Concord sport an array of rooftop solar panels. People ride bicycles or take mini-buses to work, and high-speed trains carry commuters into Boston. Everyone has cut back on meat consumption, and a radical new group, the Henry Society, includes individuals who seek to live as simply as the Concord sage. Timing is critical, for as Primack underscores, "climate change is happening now."

Although Teale could not have predicted this present crisis, he did recognize the value of Thoreau's observations, and in 1962 he published *Thoughts on Thoreau*, a compendium of excerpts lifted from the naturalist's writings and organized around themes like solitude, simplicity, society, and disobedience. He also returned to Thoreau for his final writing project. Partnering with fellow naturalist Anne Zwinger, he set out to retrace the canoe routes Thoreau had paddled on the Concord, Assabet, and Sudbury Rivers. Battling prostate cancer at the time, he drifted alongside Sudbury Meadows and reflected that "finishing the book is a kind of rounding out and completing the experience. It is, in a sense, a goodbye."

I bid farewell to Thoreau on June 12 by returning to his cabin site. The vernal pool nearby is festooned in water lilies, their petals white with specks of yellow at the center. Dragonflies hover above the surface, now covered in pollen from overhanging pitch pines. Frogs duck out of sight, and tadpoles, countless generations after Teale described them, wriggle into the depths. Thoreau sold his cabin after his two-year stay, and nine granite posts commemorate the building today. Most of the big trees that once surrounded it have been harvested, and maturing oaks offer only partial shade. The most impressive artifact is a massive stone cairn, dedicated in Thoreau's memory by Bronson Alcott and Mary Newbury Adams in 1872. Many famous naturalists, Walt Whitman, John Muir, John Burroughs, and Edwin Way Teale among them, have added to the pile. I place my offering, a piece of quartz picked up along the rail bed, atop the pyramid and depart.

Lost Elms and Flooded Fields

Mountains rise beyond Lake Champlain . . . every
grass field now has its bobolinks, fluttering and
flooding the air with song or perching on sticks or
poles. . . . Flooded fields are a sign of spring—birch-
es and elms reflected in them.

EDWIN WAY TEALE, JOURNAL OF *North with the Spring*

Teale's pursuit of spring included northern Vermont, the state
where "bobolink fields with daisies" and "large New England
elms . . . make their way in competition with other trees." Today 87 percent of the farms Edwin and Nellie drove past have
been abandoned, and 15 percent of the state's housing stock is
now devoted to tourism and recreation. Where my predecessor
discovered flooded fields, mature forests now darken the landscape. Where bobolinks once issued their "twanging, metallic-
string sound," red-tailed hawks scream and barred owls hoot.
In a work published three decades after *North with the Spring*,
Teale summarized the causes for the bobolink's decline. Not
only had pastures given way to shrubs and saplings but tractors
had replaced horses, requiring fewer hayfields and allowing for
earlier and more precise cutting. A second grassland species,
the eastern meadowlark, once "the winged embodiment of the
spirit of our spring meadows," according to John Burroughs,

has declined by more than 95 percent in Vermont since 1947. The absence of these robin-sized songsters, common across New England for generations, leaves a conspicuous gap.

"What the live oak is to the South, the American elm is to the North," Teale declared. Photographs of farmsteads from the 1940s underscore the majesty of these vase-like trees, which sheltered farmers from the heat and, according to Thoreau, offered special beauty on moonlit nights. Travelers with a sharp eye can still detect individual elms along established neighborhoods, although their iconic stature as New England's quintessential tree has been lost. Dutch elm disease, a wilt fungus spread by the elm bark beetle, entered the United States from Europe in 1928, and within four decades it had killed an estimated 100 million trees. Horticulturists in New Hampshire managed to clone a disease-resistant elm, and as a consequence, the species is making a comeback. Elms have been planted across the Northeast to take the place of white ash, itself the victim of another invasive beetle, and the American beech, preyed upon by an exotic insect and its accompanying fungus.

I spend one morning within sight of the Canadian border in the town of Newport, Vermont, whose main attraction is Lake Memphremagog. Here a female osprey calls to its mate from a nesting platform established along the lakeshore. These beautiful black-masked fish hawks have served as a harbinger of recovery in every preserve along my way. Osprey followed my kayak beyond Flamingo Harbor, plunged beneath the surf on Hunting Island, wheeled in lazy circles over Cape Cod kettle ponds, and screamed to one another across Walden Pond. The return of the osprey represents a monumental environmental victory inspired by Rachel Carson and her rebuke of the chemical industry in *Silent Spring*. As schoolchildren everywhere know, the pesticide DDT interferes with the production of calcium essential in the formation of eggshells, and keystone species like the osprey and the eagle concentrate this toxin in their tissues. By 1970 osprey numbers had plummeted by a staggering 90 percent. Dennis Puleston, a researcher who studied these birds, noted that between 1948 and 1966 the number of active nests on Gardiner's Island, New York, dwindled from over 300 to less than 50, and in these nests "we could find only four chicks." Puleston predicted "the end of the osprey as a breeding bird in the Northeast." However, once DDT was banned and new nesting platforms were erected, these fish-eating hawks gradually rebounded. Today more ospreys nest across North America than at any time in our continent's history.

Teale spent the morning of June 16 perusing the shelves of the Newport Library, a facility he found "undernourished" and "characteristic of penny-pinching New England small towns." In a remarkable turnaround, Newport today is awash in cash, thanks to a $500 million development scheme predicted to add 10,000 new jobs. A controversial federal program that offers permanent residency to any foreign investor who commits $500,000 to a rural American business is responsible for this overnight success. More than 550 wealthy individuals, most of whom live in China or Russia, have invested cash and secured these visas through a partnership with Jay Peak, a ski mountain resort 20 miles west of Newport.

Taking advantage of an early spring discount, Susie and I reserved a one-night stay at the Jay Peak Resort in May. The hotel room was beautifully appointed, with tile floors and solid maple doors. We toured the adjoining indoor ice hockey arena, where youth teams from Canada and across New England face off. We also joined guests at the indoor water park, a Disney-like facility with four waterslides, a retractable roof, and space for over 2,000 customers. The lavish resort also includes a ski mountain with seventy-six groomed trails, a championship golf course, and numerous restaurants and bars. Our waitress, a Newport native whose job was mandated by these federal incentives, expressed skepticism about whether the program's promised returns will, in fact, materialize.

The next morning we hiked to the summit of South Gilpin Mountain along the Long Trail. Trout lilies and trillium alternated with patches of snow, and we paused to listen to the beautiful song of the winter wren and the muffled whirr of a ruffed grouse. Near the summit we came upon an open area in the forest where moose had taken shelter—piles of scat and browsed low branches documented their temporary stay. Like eagles and osprey, these ungainly herbivores have staged a dramatic comeback in Vermont, New Hampshire, and Maine as forest cover expands and wetlands return. Beavers, another species wiped out in the 1800s and still rare when Teale traveled, have played a key role in expanding habitat for moose. And while beaver numbers continue to increase, the moose population across New England has suddenly declined by some 40 percent. The explosive growth of deer ticks as temperatures warm appears to be the cause.

On his way through Vermont to Lake Champlain, Teale passed "brimming brooks and flooded lowland meadows." Evidence of extensive flooding abounds in my travels through Vermont as well: single-lane roads parallel streambeds, and detours bypass flood-damaged culverts. Tropical Storm Irene devastated Vermont the previous August, dumping 7 inches of rain across central counties in a matter of hours. Such slow-moving supersaturated tropical depressions like Irene, and Superstorm Sandy the following year, are harbingers of what the Northeast can expect in the years ahead. Fed by warming ocean currents, storms like these have forced officials in Vermont to confront a new future—one that will require moving roads away from rivers, resizing culverts, and ultimately denying requests to rebuild in flood-prone areas. As Vermont's own Bill McKibben has concluded: "We've built a new Eaarth. It's not as nice as the old one; it's the greatest mistake humans have ever made, one that we will pay for literally forever."

I follow Teale over the causeway to Grand Isle and North Hero on my way to visit Isle La Motte. Kingbirds perch on telephone wires, and goldfinches, identified by their "rocking-horse flight," wing among the sycamores. Only 7 miles long and 3 miles wide, Isle La Motte is home to one of the oldest limestone reefs on earth. Stone quarried here was transported as far away as New York City and Washington, D.C., where it was used to embellish Radio City Music Hall and the National Gallery of Art. The priceless "flaws" in this gray-black limestone result from fossilized sea creatures—some of them nearly half a billion years old. At the Fisk Quarry Preserve, I pick my way among shallow pools and look out across immense tablelands. The stone beneath my feet reveals primitive snail whirls and twig-shaped forms of even earlier sea creatures. Plate tectonics eons ago account for the reef's northern location, and signage here describes not only the geology and history of quarrying operations but also the efforts of Linda Fitch, who singlehandedly fought to protect the site.

In mid-June I schedule a second foray to central Vermont to visit John Elder, professor emeritus at Middlebury College, co-editor of the *Norton Anthology of Nature Writing*, and author of three books focused on New England's natural history. In one of these he offers his impressions of Vermont's vernal season: "Because it is so brief and so intense, spring in Vermont, like the brooks along the heights, may escape notice. . . . I won't be open to it if I have to wait for warmth, or for leaves on the trees."

John lives in Bristol, a mill village of 3,800 residents located along the New Haven River. We walk to the end of his street and climb the winding wooded trail along Hogback Ridge to the Bristol Ledges that overlook the valley below. The steep slope of underlying bedrock prevented this 10-mile stretch from

Isle La Motte quarry in Lake Champlain. Photo by author.

being settled or later developed. However, he and his neighbors have become concerned now that the technology exists to blast and build second homes almost anywhere. They have recently banded together with a regional land trust to protect Bristol Ledges from residential development. Local nonprofit entities like land trusts now form the backbone of Vermont's conservation efforts.

Stone walls crisscross the Bristol Ledges summit, indicating that sheep were once pastured at this height. More than a million Merinos browsed Vermont hillsides in 1840, after William Jarvis, ambassador to Portugal, secretly exported them to his Wethersfield farm 80 miles to the south. Their overgrazing created an ecological nightmare, which George Perkins Marsh, who lived in nearby Woodstock, first called attention to in 1864. History is local in this small state, John assures me, and *North with the Spring*, together with Aldo Leopold's *Sand County Almanac*, the photographs of Ansel Adams, and the rediscovery of Henry David Thoreau, helped raise Americans' awareness of nature in the 1950s. "Teale's highlighting of wild places accessible by automobiles dovetailed perfectly with the mood of the country following World War II," he says. This enthusiasm galvanized support for passage of the wilderness preservation acts and expansion of the National Park Service a decade later. John credits Rachel Carson with preparing the way for the Clean Water and Clean Air Acts of the following decade, and he highlights the tireless efforts of his friend Bill McKibben to alert Americans to the challenges of global warming. My friend concludes this synopsis by noting that "the voices of earlier naturalists like Burroughs, Beston, Teale, and John Hay continue to offer much of value even, or especially, at this present moment of global crisis."

As the sun sinks, a hermit thrush begins its flutelike refrain in the woods behind us. "This bird never fails to speak to me out of an ether purer than that I breathe," Thoreau had written, and Teale had called attention to its melodious notes in his chapter on springtime in northern Vermont. Excited, John asks if I know the Frost poem about the thrush, and while listening to its song, he recites all five stanzas. "I love that phrase 'Far in the pillared dark / Thrush music went,'" he says as we shoulder our packs and descend.

Vermont's governor, Peter Shumlin, has pledged that the state will generate 90 percent of its total energy requirements from renewable sources by 2050. Wind power forms one element of his vision for sustainability, and massive turbines atop Vermont ridgelines have sparked fierce controversy. John Elder has become embroiled in this issue by voicing his support for a proposed wind farm with 400-foot towers in Searsburg and Readsboro. Like many others, he argues for the region's need to wean itself from reliance on fossil fuels and foreign governments. At the same time, he understands the fierce attachment Vermonters have for unspoiled vistas and roadless preserves. Energy debates pit neighbor against neighbor and are resolved through face-to-face discussions and a show of local hands. Town meetings, held throughout Vermont on a single day in March, still serve the democratic principles they were designed to protect.

A Second Longest Day

At the cabin, we started a fire of birchwood in the
fireplace, sat in the warmth and flickering light, talking of our great good fortune and the long adventure
we had shared together. . . . The longest day of the
year was over and night was come—stars shone all
over the clear sky. June 21st was almost over and so
was spring. For us, there would never be another
spring like this one in all our lives.

Edwin Way Teale, Journal of *North with the Spring*

From rattlesnakes in Florida to stinkpots in Virginia, Teale delighted in handling reptiles throughout his excursion. Therefore, as June draws to a close, I schedule a meeting with David
M. Carroll, affectionately known as the "turtle man" across
New England. Entranced by these reptiles at a very early age,
David, who lives in Warner, New Hampshire, has spent his
life slogging through wetlands to learn the mysteries of their
ways. A modern-day Thoreau—weathered, stubborn, sufficiently talented to have received a MacArthur "genius grant"—
he devotes spring, summer, and fall to tracking turtles, and he
spends his winter months writing, painting, and philosophiz-
ing. He's become something of an extremist in his stance on
preservation: "What will be regarded by nearly everyone as a

conservation victory, a cause for celebration, I can see only as loss and sorrow."

We spend the morning together in the 1,000-acre sanctuary David has named the "Digs." Here we walk along the edge of a hayfield searching for wood turtles, a northern species with a rough, keeled shell, bright orange legs, and sharp-clawed feet. Wood turtles migrate to the forest edge from their nearby river to bask in the sun and feed on slugs and other insects that emerge after rain. From years of practice, David knows their resting places, and in half an hour we locate a dozen wood turtles of various sizes. He is particularly excited to reacquaint himself with the forty-five-year-old "alpha male," the main breeder in this population, and with a five-year-old male, according to its plastron rings, that is new to him. He takes time to measure and weigh this new turtle, to sketch its carapace, and to score one corner of its shell with a tiny file.

Later that morning we strap on waders and plunge into a reed canary grass swamp in a different section of the Digs. As David stops to study the water's surface, I'm reminded of Wordsworth's old leech-gatherer wandering alone across desolate moors. Within minutes, David makes a quick lunge and brings to the surface a beautifully marbled black and yellow spotted turtle. This dome-shaped jewel, about the size of a watch box, is familiar to him, and he hands her to me with remarkable tenderness. Spotted turtles seldom leave the swamp where they are born except to nest, and females deposit their eggs in small clutches of five to seven. It's an absolute thrill to hold something so stunningly elegant, so rarely seen, so ancient, and yet so vulnerable.

David had hoped the Digs would receive special covenants beyond the typical conservation easement. He had argued for absolute restrictions, a sanctuary model like that embraced at Tupper Hill, where he had been invited to study turtle populations years before. Purchased by the Norcross Foundation, Tupper Hill in rural Massachusetts features 5,000 acres of protected land, only 20 of which are open to the public. The remaining fields, forests, and wetlands, 99 percent of the sanctuary, are off-limits to all except a handful of experts.

"Why," he asks me over lunch, "is such a true setting-aside for nature so rare in the global landscape?" When I mention the future vision for the U.S. Fish and Wildlife Service, David groans. Their plan to offer expanded access at many federal sanctuaries sounds to him like yet another compromise—one designed to recruit funds and accommodate humans at the expense of wild creatures like his turtles. He would prefer to close all federal refuges—to turn back the clock to the time when restrictions first began. "Keep the Okefenokee Swamp for the turtles, not the tourists!" he insists. A visit to his art studio reveals watercolor paintings of spotted turtles set in beautiful Japanese motifs. At present the spotted turtle is endangered in Vermont, threatened in Maine, and of special concern in Massachusetts and New Hampshire.

Teale's experience with Venus flytraps, burrowing owls, and Hessel's hairstreaks made him sensitive to the plight of endangered species. In *North with the Spring* he tells the story of John Muir, who "half a century ago . . . tried to buy a section of prairie land at his boyhood farm in Wisconsin, hoping to turn it into a sanctuary where the pasque-flower would bloom in the spring and conditions that existed in pioneer times would be maintained." Although Muir was unsuccessful, Teale held out hope for what he called "type specimen" sanctuaries. After all, he wrote, "habitat areas, as well as species of birds and wildflowers, can become extinct."

✦ ✦ ✦

"The spruce and fir and balsam trees that cover the hilltops mark the character of the land. They are the badge of the north country." Edwin and Nellie spent several days exploring the White Mountains of New Hampshire, for in these high elevations they were able to continue their pursuit of "a far-northern spring—a tardier, shorter, speedier season." This region of the state maintains a 1950s feel, for the land itself remains the central character. The same roads parallel riverbeds, the identical trails wind up mountain slopes, and many of the hotels they mentioned still welcome visitors. With a bit of luck, Susie and I locate a cluster of roadside cabins almost identical to those where my predecessor spent the night. Set along a gentle slope just off of Route 302, these cottages—once available for $4 and now reserved for $90—offer a similar view "across the level of the valley to the heights of the mountains to the east." The tiny kitchen, narrow sitting room, and 10 by 12 foot bedroom give us a taste for the comfort and "great good fortune" my mentor experienced as he wrote the chapter epigraph. We too sit on the porch after sunset, listening to the rustle of aspen leaves and the whistle of the white-throated sparrow.

A close reading of Teale's journals reveals that even here much has changed. The Fabyan House where Edwin watched "bank swallows sporting in the dusk," and where up to 500 guests once vacationed, burned to the ground in 1951. The famous Willey House, where a family of seven was killed attempting to flee a rockslide in 1826, included a cabin site where the Teales stayed. Today, the Willey House is marked by a simple plaque, a souvenir station, and a set of public restrooms. The naturalist noted "short pulp-paper logs stranded on the rocks along the length" of the Androscoggin River. These were some of the last logs to float that river, for paper manufacturing in the North Country began its agonizing slow decline shortly after World War II. The massive mills positioned along the Androscoggin closed their doors one by one, and when the smokestacks finally came down in 2007, to Berlin residents "the change felt like death."

Susie and I visit Clark's Trading Post, the tourist destination where Teale had marveled as captive bears pulled on a rope "which functions like an apartment-house clothes line" to retrieve a can of peanuts. I remember the poles, platforms, and ingenious pulley system from my visit to the North Country as a boy. However, animal rights activists put an end to that spectacle, and today the bears entertain by rolling balls and climbing towers in a makeshift arena. They share the stage with newer forms of amusement: a Segway safari, blaster boats, Chinese acrobats, and a train ride to Merlin's mansion.

On June 21, the final day of spring, Edwin awoke an hour before dawn. He listened to robins "begin their matins," heard the song of an oven bird, and trilled to his favorite, a white-throated sparrow. For months the couple had planned to ascend Mount Washington via the Cog Railway on this, the longest day of the year. Here, an ascent above tree line "would coincide with the advance of spring as far north as Hudson Bay." I'd formulated a different plan for the final day of spring, my wife's birthday, imagining a picnic lunch at Trail Wood, the central Connecticut retreat where the Teales had lived out their years. Late in his life Edwin devoted two books to the study of phenology at Trail Wood, and so it seemed fitting to conclude my journey there.

However, the morning of June 21, 2012, dawns hot and humid, with predictions to reach 95 degrees across New England. Susie suggests that we drive north to escape the heat, and so I hastily substitute the summit of Mount Washington. When we arrive at the base of the mountain around 10 a.m., the temperature has already climbed above 80 degrees. Dozens of sightseers await the Cog, advertised as the oldest man-made tourist attraction in North America. Our tickets cost ten times what my predecessor paid. The ticket counter, filled with historic photographs, is familiar, for we had hoped to take my father to the summit before his vision failed. Dense fog that day grounded the train.

Across from the arrival platform, a swallowtail butterfly feeds on the last of the lilac blossoms, while a single monarch hovers in search of nectar. Teale kept his meticulous eye out for monarchs and recorded their passage again and again:

"We see monarchs drifting aimlessly along the Suwannee River . . . at the edge of the Okefenokee Swamp, . . . among the barrier islands of South Carolina, . . . amid the pitch pines of the New Jersey barrens, . . . and along New England rivers." Entomologists after World War II knew only part of the monarch's migration story. Males and females had been documented in equal numbers during fall migration, while in the spring mostly females traveled back north alone. Edwin and Nellie had witnessed thousands of monarchs settling for the night close to their Long Island home, and they were aware that "tens of thousands of monarch butterflies congregate on cypress trees" in California's Pacific Grove. But no one knew for sure where most of these colonies spent the winter.

In 1976 Dr. Fred Urquhart, a Canadian zoologist who had tracked these charismatic insects since 1937, documented innumerable monarchs within "scarcely twenty acres on a lofty wooded slope in central Mexico." Urquhart enlisted the support of more than 1,000 volunteer observers, and one of these trackers reported seeing a large concentration of monarchs crisscrossing the Sierra Madre region of Mexico. The following winter Urquhart hiked along the mountain crest to a clearing surrounded by oyamel trees, a boreal species of fir. There he described a sea of orange: "In the quietness of semi-dormancy, they festooned the tree branches, they enveloped the oyamel trees, they carpeted the ground in their tremulous legions." Like other insects, monarchs adjust their body temperature to the surrounding ambient air, and in this remote 9,000-foot location winter temperatures hover just above or just below freezing. Rendered dormant by the chill, monarchs consume only a tiny percentage of the fat reserves they put on in the fall and will require for their journey north in the spring.

As many as 1 billion monarchs were estimated to overwinter in the central Mexican highlands when Urquhart made his discovery. Twenty years later, the Mexican government established a Monarch Butterfly Biosphere Reserve to help protect these vulnerable colonies. Unfortunately, in recent decades monarch numbers have plummeted, and entomologists suspect several factors are at work. Illegal logging has reduced the size of the reserve; extensive applications of herbicides like Roundup have eliminated midwestern milkweed plants; and severe weather has become more common, including droughts with temperatures above 95 degrees across Texas and extreme late spring snowstorms. Like canaries in the coal mine, monarchs appear to be harbingers of our threatened future. In 2012 the numbers of these butterflies across New England declined by a staggering 60 percent.

Powered by one of the Cog's new diesel locomotives, we begin our 3-mile climb. The ride up the mountain proved "unpleasant, fatiguing, and nerve-strung" for my predecessor, whose sharp eyes noted a patch of black earth signifying an earlier accident. By contrast, Susie and I feel elated, pleased to be rising above the heat and in the company of others who appreciate the meticulous detailing of this new coach's interior. Once past the antiquated water tower, we look back on the valley where "yellow birch grow almost up to timberline," and then ahead at the Krummholz or "crooked wood," a thick mat of dwarfed balsam fir and black spruce. As we approach the summit, clouds move in, the wind picks up, and a barren landscape of lichen-covered rock replaces the patchwork of green.

We step out into dense fog and are buffeted by 50 mph winds and temperatures below 60 degrees. Clad in summer attire—shorts and a sundress—we hug each other and bend into the gusts. Inside the Sherman Adams Visitor Center, a raucous group of thru hikers exchange stories at a table nearby. Fortified by cheese, salami, and a birthday toast of champagne, we wander downstairs to the museum exhibits. The displays highlight the geology of the White Mountains, the history of summit construction, the record of extreme weather events, and the wildlife that calls this foreboding mountain home. One diorama depicts the rare Bicknell's thrush, the most secretive member of the thrush family, which prefers to nest in balsam fir and red spruce forests above 3,000 feet. Teale actually heard one of these rare songsters on the summit during his visit in June. The thrushes' numbers have declined at an annual rate of about 7 percent for the last twenty years, and almost half of the entire American Bicknell's population now nests exclusively in the White Mountains. Atmospheric pollution from coal-fired power plants and climatic warming across New England, along with deforestation and habitat loss in its wintering grounds in the Dominican Republic and Haiti, have hastened the birds' demise. According to a report by the International Bicknell's Thrush Conservation Group, warming temperatures of as little as 1 degree Celsius could further reduce the birds' habitat by more than half. A 3 degree increase in spring temperatures would likely eliminate this species from across the Northeast. And because summer temperatures are now expected to rise between 2.8 and 5.9 degrees Celsius by 2100, the Bicknell's is listed as one of the most threatened passerines in eastern North America.

Back outside, a stark, alien landscape of rock and mist envelops us. We walk beyond the Tip Top House, a squat stone structure built in 1853, and notice a tiny splash of white—Diapensia in full bloom, and further out the magenta flowers of the Lapland rosebay. In its heyday, Mount Washington offered visitors five bridle paths as well as a carriage road to guesthouses and spacious hotels on the summit. Henry David Thoreau became concerned about this privatization: "I think that the top of Mount Washington should not be private property; it should be left unappropriated for modesty and reverence's sake, or if only to suggest that earth has higher uses than we put her to." Part of the White Mountain National Forest, the peak of Mount Washington remains littered with structures and scarred by a road that offers access to more than 45,000 cars each year. As we prepare to make our descent, I offer Susie a second toast—to continued good health, to our delightful

On Mount Washington's summit with my wife, Susie. Photo by author.

marriage, and to the successful completion of my odyssey in the footsteps of Edwin Way Teale.

New Hampshire's most famous tourist attraction used to be the Old Man of the Mountain. "In the evening light, the form of this majestic natural monument, set above the reflecting pool beneath it, seems a superb example of nature's artistry," Teale wrote on their way homeward. However, on May 3, 2003, the stone face let go, leaving some 7,200 tons of granite piled beneath Cannon Mountain. Thousands of people mourned the loss of this icon, and as a result a private group of admirers raised $250,000 to install seven "profilers," sleek metal poles positioned so that their sculpted tips might re-create the form of the Old Man's craggy visage. We elect not to stop, preferring Teale's poignant description and our own vivid memories.

Reluctant to end their affair with spring, the Teales spent the night of June 22 at Miller's Falls, Massachusetts, and dawdled further the next afternoon. Within a few miles of their Baldwin home, he drove "east to Freeport, then south across the causeway to Jones Beach and on and on east until eventually we came to the end and the final turnaround." Although I once imagined the ghost of David as responsible for this pause, after traveling in Edwin's footsteps for almost four months, I feel certain that gratitude, not anguish, accounts for his "nearly a hundred mile" delay.

The publication of *North with the Spring* four years later solidified Edwin Way Teale's reputation as America's preeminent natural history writer during the 1950s. And long before the close of their adventure, he sensed the promise in that volume. His field notes totaled more than 400,000 words, and with Nellie beside him, he had traveled more than 17,000 miles. His journal entries indicate his eagerness to begin the book, for the dark moods of February had finally given way to joy. A simple turn of the key put an end to their adventure. For me, however, arriving home was not sufficient. One more destination, the place where Edwin ultimately felt most at home, still beckoned.

....18

Blessed Trail Wood

> In a little while most of this band of northward
> moving warblers will be gone from these woods. In
> a little while longer they will be gone from the earth.
> Their species will continue on but they as individuals
> are—as are all the forms of life the world contains—
> transients. This the rational mind sees, realizes, ac-
> cepts. . . . But the heart still longs for the impossible;
> for more and more life, for life unending. It wants
> the warblers to stay with us, to fill the woods with
> their bright colors and their bright songs forever.
>
> EDWIN WAY TEALE, *A Walk through the Year*

Teale penned these words thirty years after he and Nellie completed their glorious adventure with spring. The woods he
speaks of is Trail Wood, the sanctuary he long desired in emu-
lation of Jefferson's Monticello or Marjorie Kinnan Rawlings'
Cross Creek home. The couple moved to this 80-acre parcel in
Hampton, Connecticut, a decade after *North with the Spring*
appeared. In those intervening years they traveled almost
40,000 miles in two more transcontinental excursions. At Trail
Wood Edwin would construct a gazebo dedicated to Nellie and
fashion a writer's cabin for himself modeled upon Thoreau's.
Together with his books, this sanctuary would serve as their
enduring legacy, for without an heir, the couple decided to

donate their home to the Connecticut Audubon Society once they were gone.

In addition to a compact 1806 Cape Cod house, set on a knoll, the property includes a parking area, a pond, and a work shed that functions as its education center. A poster pinned above the blackboard reads: "Trail Wood, blessed Trail Wood, is just the same. No place on earth that we have seen appeals to us more." It is signed EWT and dated March 26, 1962. Following paths the owners cleared and later named, I stop beside a cairn in Monument Pasture, where dandelions are going to seed, and wander among the oaks and hickories along Fern Brook Trail. I pause at Hyla Pond, now bone dry in the record summer heat, and follow the tracks of horses along Old Colonial Road, which marks the northern terminus of their property. Turning south at Big Grapevine Trail, I pass in and out of sunlight until I catch a glimpse of a narrow wooden bridge. Across the sunken pond covered in water lilies sits the screened gazebo, and I have little trouble imagining Nellie inside, scanning the water's surface and keeping a watchful eye on the cabin where her pensive husband writes.

Set on a stone foundation, a dozen rough-hewn logs support a cedar-shake roof. Windows bring light in from every direction, and a faint footpath still connects the nearby woods. "Rubber flippers . . . snowshoes . . . a rusted rapier . . . a worn insect collecting net" decorate the interior walls, while "colored rocks . . . a stomach stone . . . a fragment of Indian pottery . . . and the skull of a kit fox" adorn the bookshelf. The pack basket David made long ago hangs above the desk. Trail Wood helped Edwin achieve the balance he so desired, for as the epigraph indicates, he was able finally to acknowledge both transience and everlasting life. The volume that describes this maturation, *A Naturalist Buys an Old Farm,* ends on an optimistic note. "Sitting under the apple trees, walking down the lane, following the wood trails, circling the pond at sunset, our life here has seemed all kernel and no husk."

As is often the case with a writer, the unpublished autobiographical journals record a different story. "Always hereafter, on this Saturday in June, the fifteenth day of the month in the year of 1974, will seem the watershed, the great divide of my life." On this day Edwin received news that his test for prostate cancer had come back positive. His first thought, of course, was for Nellie: "A note to myself. In times of strain and tragedy, I tend to endure by withdrawing into myself. Avoid this now. I have always regretted that I endured David's loss—so overwhelming—in this way. I should help Nellie get through in every way I can."

Because he feared the worst in this diagnosis, Edwin began to scale back his latest writing project, *A Journey through the Year*, envisioning a "smaller book," one entitled "A Journey through the Spring." However, the cancer proved to be slow growing, and he was able to complete this catalogue of seasonal observations and then begin a new project, his collaboration with Anne Zwinger paying homage to Thoreau. Nellie kept her own diary of events at Trail Wood. Less formal and philosophical than Edwin's, her entries, often scribbled into small 3 × 5 lined booklets, intersperse shopping lists, notes on the season's progress, and comments on her husband's deteriorating health. During the final month of his life Nellie remained at his bedside constantly, reading to him and holding his hand. She slept in the hospital library and ventured home only to nap and shower. She was away on one of these rare occasions at Trail Wood on the afternoon of October 18, 1980, when he died.

As instructed, Nellie buried half of Edwin's ashes in the grave and sprinkled the other half at his favorite observation posts around Trail Wood. Her final thoughts on the day she laid her husband to rest move out beyond her current grief: "I feel him near all the time—He left me with so many wonderful memories and he left such a great legacy in his books. Human memory can fade—or go from us—but the written word

Resting place of Edwin and Nellie Teale, North Cemetery, Hampton, Connecticut. Photo by author.

endures as long as it can be preserved. In this age of nuclear force in the hands of humans, our civilization as we know it can be wiped out—destroyed. Our beautiful earth can be destroyed. We hope this will never happen, but the possibility is very real."

"Our beautiful earth can be destroyed." The source of the threat has changed, but the consequences remain the same. As Elizabeth Kolbert reminds us, "Right now, in the amazing moment that to us counts as the present, we are deciding, without quite meaning to, which evolutionary pathways will remain open and which will forever be closed." Humanity has never before had such power, and given the predictions, is unlikely to ever have it again. The Teales prayed for an end to the Cold War, but in the meantime they acted—returning again and again to what inspired them and working with others to preserve and protect the places they loved. The stakes are higher today, but the actions remain the same. We have an opportunity to witness the incredible natural beauty that still surrounds us and an obligation to reduce the impact of the sixth extinction for all of those who are threatened, including ourselves.

More than anyone of his generation, Edwin understood and loved the fragile interrelationships among plants, insects, birds, animals, and people in the places where they lived. Nellie assisted her husband to see these connections and channeled her compassion and wisdom into helping him express them. They lie buried side by side in the northeast corner of Hampton North Cemetery. The moment I stepped from the car, I recognized their slate stone positioned beside a rock wall and shaded by three tall Norway spruces. A robin stands etched in relief along the top, and flowering vines decorate either side. David, too, is with them, for the lower half of the tombstone reads: "Died in Germany on the Moselle River. Buried in the Military Cemetery Margraten, Holland." The final sentence this remarkable couple chose forms a fitting close:

Two who loved this earth
and loved each other.

Acknowledgments

Many people have helped at various stages in the production of this book, and to each of them I offer my sincere thanks. I am especially indebted to the following individuals who served as guides in the field and readers of the manuscript: Jane Brox, Gerald Burns, David M. Carroll, Dennis and Maureen Darcy, Debbie Donley, John Elder, Win Everham, Robert Finch, Dr. Paul Gray, Jeff Hoffman, Ken Huser, Louisa Kerwin, John Lane and Betsy Teter, Chris Lowie, Tricia Lynch, David McLean, Tom and Lynn Nash, Johnny Randall, Janisse Ray and Raven Waters, Dawna Standridge, John and Robin Stronk, Anne McCrary Sullivan, Richard Telford, and Jim and Sasha Wohlpart.

The chapter on the Ducktown Desert originally appeared in the magazine *Natural History*, and I wish to convey my appreciation to David Harris. In addition, the Monadnock Institute of Nature, Place, and Culture at Franklin Pierce University and the Whiting Foundation provided important support for the project. I am also indebted to Hannah Oxley for her mapmaking skills, Melissa Waterworth Batt for her comprehensive knowledge of the Edwin Way Teale manuscript collection at the University of Connecticut, Melissa Stearns for her excellent index, and my editors Sian Hunter, Sonia Dickey, and Nevil Parker at the University Press of Florida.

Notes

Abbreviations

JNWS   Journal of *North with the Spring*
NWS   *North with the Spring*

Chapter 1. Plotting the Course

4   to trace *"firsthand"*: NWS, 2.
4   *"We first smelled smoke"*: NWS, 4.
4   *"was more up and down"*: Millard C. Davis, "Interview with Nellie Teale," August 4, 1990, Teale Papers, box 230, folder 5375.
5   *"the most congenial person still"*: NWS, 3.
5   *"I shall be frank Mrs. Teale"*: Letter from Nellie Donovan to Clara Teale, November 8, 1922, Teale Papers, series III, box 146.
5   *"a speedy, glamorous escape"*: Paes de Barros, 228.
5   *Fifty-four percent*: Rugh, 12.
5   *"We meet no man-eating bears"*: Teale, "Adventures in Making a Living, 1941–51," Teale Papers, box 113.
7   *"maps . . . bird glasses"*: NWS, 3.

Chapter 2. The Wildest Place

8   *"with their piercing 'Kee-You' whistle"*: JNWS, vol. 1, part 1, 57.
8   *"a copper-burnished sunset"*: JNWS, vol. 1, part 1, 44.
9   *"leaving everyday responsibilities behind"*: NWS, 2.
9   *"belief and optimism"*: NWS, 14.
9   *"only this we know"*: JNWS, vol. 1, part 1, 64.
11   memorialized in her poem *"Holding On"*: Sullivan, 15.
13   *"every store and every business building"*: JNWS, vol. 1, part 1, 61.
14   *"bridled and balkanized"*: Levin, 3.

17   *"swallows milling in clouds"*: NWS, 10.

17   *"low choral thunder"*: Sullivan, 27.

19   *"Things are seldom as they seem"*: Orlean, 9.

19   *"to learn from the limestone"*: Sullivan, 77.

20   *the rate of sea-level rise*: Douglas, 451; Florida Oceans and Coastal Council report.

Chapter 3. Restoring Our Losses

22   *"whose rhythms and pulse"*: Weidensaul, 79.

23   *"on the great hurricane embankment"*: JNWS, vol. 1, part 1, 91.

23   *"water-level recording instruments"*: JNWS, vol. 1, part 1, 98.

23   *"paddling together among bulrushes"*: JNWS, vol. 1, part 1, 108.

23   *"man's music is almost unbearable"*: JNWS, vol. 2, part 2, 30.

24   *"down winding trails"*: NWS, 32.

24   *"snow-white masses"* and *"pearlike eggs"*: NWS, 33.

24   *"the outlandish calling of the limpkins"*: NWS, 37–38.

25   *water hyacinths, Florida gallinules*: JNWS, vol. 1, part 1, 95.

27   *"bobbing little burrowing owls"*: NWS, 39.

30   *"the largest alligator I had ever seen"*: NWS, 140.

30   *"participatory state of mind"*: Livingston, 17.

32   *"banded ten times as many eagles"*: JNWS, vol. 1, part 1, 121.

32   *"an eagle's nest about every mile"*: JNWS, vol. 1, part 1, 123.

32   *"Mr. Broley ranged"*: Carson, 118–19.

34   *"Ultimately, the future of a natural ecosystem"*: Jordan, 16.

34   *"achieve awareness of the other"*: Jordan, 51.

34   *"language of action and performance"*: Jordan, 51.

34   *"open-ended exchange"*: Jordan, 52

34   *"deepening sense of ambiguity"*: Jordan, 52.

34   *"The act of restoration"*: Jordan, 73.

36   *"the rewilding not only"*: MacKinnon, 157.

36   *"'North' . . . is a Thoreauvian ramble,"* Chidester presentation.

36   *"killdeers nesting"*: Win Everham, e-mail to John Harris, March 22, 2012.

Chapter 4. Song of the Cardinal

38   *"luscious and fruitful, . . . newly minted land"*: Orlean, 123.

38   *"long slow drive racked by washboards"*: NWS, 25.

38–39 *"burnished and clear"*: JNWS, vol. 1, part 1, 68.

39   *"the solitude and wild beaches"*: Ding Darling National Wildlife Refuge Narrative Report 1967, 22.

40   *"a rusting mass of boilers"*: JNWS, vol. 1, part 1, 57.

40   *Gator hunting*: Ogden, 78.

40   *"a great blinding white beach"*: JNWS, vol. 1, part 1, 46.

40   *"a large black sow"*: JNWS, vol. 1, part 1, 47.

41   *"the loneliest cemetery"*: JNWS, vol. 1, part 1, 48.

41   *"one so modern"*: JNWS, vol. 1, part 1, 48.

42   *"something sacred reveals itself"*: Lopez, 228.

42   *"strange and eerie"*: JNWS, vol. 1, part 2, 32.

42   *"thick raft of hyacinths"*: JNWS, vol. 1, part 2, 34.

42   *"amphitheater of trees"*: JNWS, vol. 1, part 2, 34.

42   *Cowkeeper welcomed Bartram*: Bartram, 165.

43   *"mind seemed dried out, hardened like putty"*: NWS, 25.

44   *"I was glad at the thought"*: NWS, 27.

46   *"secret and lovely place"*: NWS, 59.

46   *"boiled halves of grapefruit"*: NWS, 57.

46   *"She is generous in the extreme"*: JNWS, vol. 1, part 2, 15.

47   *"Life now stirs and sap rises"*: Rawlings, 256–57.

47   *a letter he read in a Florida newspaper*: NWS, 115; also see Mooallem, "American Hippopotamus."

48   *"tinge of green"* and *"infinitesimal rosy"*: Rawlings, 257.

48   *"pair of red-birds"*: Rawlings, 379.

48   *"a fresh, free, unspoiled start"*: Orlean, 123.

48   *"Thousands of idle loungers"*: Levin, 190.

49   *"is not some injured"*: Finch, *Death of a Hornet*, 121.

Chapter 5. Drowned Circular Chasms

50   *"pure, transparent . . . untainted by salt"*: NWS, 89.

51   *"Silver Springs' flow will stop"*: "Florida Struggles," *New York Times*, June 22, 2012.

51   *"these stressors are changing the ecology"*: Howard T. Odum Florida Springs Institute, *Silver Springs Ecosystem Study (2012–2013)*, 3. http://floridaspringsinstitute.org/Resources/Documents/Annual_Report_%202013.pdf.

52   *offered a $100 prize*: JNWS, vol. 1, part 1, 140.

53   *"wildcat that hissed, growled"*: JNWS, vol. 1, part 2, 44.

54   *"astonishing ebullition"*: Bartram, 198–99.

54   *"Five manatees swam into the bay"*: JNWS, vol. 1, part 1, 40.

55   *"vast plain of water"* and following: Bartram, 168–69.

55   *"entrance to these 'gopher' holes"*: NWS, 66.

57   *"One of the shyest of southern swamp birds"*: NWS, 90.

57   *"regained the fearlessness"*: NWS, 91.

58   *"That evening the dusk was filled"*: NWS, 90.

58   *weather was the more likely culprit*: Bryan, "Wakulla Timeline."

58   *"Nothing depresses me more"*: JNWS, vol. 1, part 2, 61.

59   *"more than half of their current climatic range"*: Barringer, "Climate Change Will Disrupt," *New York Times*, September 8, 2014.

59   *"It was the voice of the dark, the swamp"*: NWS, 91.

60   *"Tho' much is taken, much abides"*: Lord Alfred Tennyson, "Ulysses" (1842), line 65.

Chapter 6. Land of Trembling Earth

61   *"curtains behind curtains"*: NWS, 134.

62   *"This is the most interesting park I know"*: JNWS, vol. 1, part 2, 113.

62   *The photograph he took*: NWS, opposite 141.

65   *"in a country where 100,66,66 acres"*: NWS, 134.

66   *"first beaver since the refuge"*: Okefenokee National Wildlife Refuge Narrative Report, 1969, 6.

66   *"big and raw-boned"*: JNWS, vol. 1, part 2, 119.

66   *"only its eyes"*: JNWS, vol. 1, part 2, 114.

67   *only 8 percent of nested alligator eggs hatched*: Okefenokee National Wildlife Refuge Narrative Report, 1975, 28.

68   *"They hauled him into the boat"*: Hamp Mizell, in Harper and Presley, 72.

70   *I recall Teale's photo*: NWS, opposite 76.

70   *"chopped or sawed"*: JNWS, vol. 1, part 2, 127.

70   *"Nothing is more beautiful"*: Ray, 14.

71   *"disagreeable, penetrating odors"*: JNWS, vol. 1, part 2, 127

71   *"poorer filling stations"*: JNWS, vol. 1, part 2, 110.

71   *"The policeman walked past"*: JNWS, vol. 1, part 2, 110.

72   *"tin shacks and wooden racks"*: JNWS, vol. 1, part 2, 131.

72   *visit the natural history museum*: JNWS, vol. 1, part 2, 133.

73   *"never recall such a peculiar"*: JNWS, vol. 1, part 2, 135.

73   *"no nesting activities"*: JNWS, vol. 1, part 2, 135.

73   *"most becoming American city"*: Bryson, 83.

73   *complained of clogged intersections*: JNWS, vol. 1, part 2, 135–40.

73   *"hardly one alligator"*: JNWS, vol. 1, part 2, 135.

Chapter 7. A Splendid, Unforgettable Week

74   *"guilty feelings for all that David"*: JNWS, vol. 1, part 2, 138–39.

74   *"Mecca for naturalists"*: NWS, 137.

75   *"two of the most congenial people"*: NWS, 142.

75   *"a splendid, unforgettable week"*: JNWS, vol. 1, part 3, 55.

76   *"little heaps and windrows"*: JNWS, vol. 1, part 3, 40.

77   *"silvery snakes of inlet rivers"*: JNWS, vol. 1, part 3, 40.

78   *"fern-bearing and hoary"*: JNWS, vol. 1, part 3, 19.

79   *"600 loggerhead egg nests"*: NWS, 139.

79   *"the big sight of the day"*: JNWS, vol. 1, part 3, 12.

80   *"half-buried wreck of a ship"*: JNWS, vol. 1, part 3, 21–22.

80 *"the scattered skeletons"*: JNWS, vol. 1, part 3, 21–22.

80 *"accumulated almost 30 ticks"*: JNWS, vol. 1, part 3, 38.

80 *"one of the most heavily infested spots"*: NWS, 145.

81 *"little fenced-in plot"*: JNWS, vol. 1, part 3, 33.

81 *"loneliest cemetery since Marco Island"*: JNWS, vol. 1, part 3, 33.

82 *"would never be the same again"*: JNWS, vol. 1, part 2, 137.

82 *"I imagine this is the strangest"*: letter from Edwin Teale to David Teale, April 1, 1945, Teale Papers, series III, box 145, folder 2942.

82 *"the wonderful example of love"*: letter from David Teale to his mother, November 2, 1944, Teale Papers, series III, box 146, folder 2949.

82 *"matters straightened at home"*: letter from David Teale to his parents, December 17, 1944, Teale Papers, series III, box 146, folder 2949.

83 *"such a letter as I did"*: letter from David Teale to his parents, December 24, 1944, Teale Papers, series III, box 146, folder 2949.

83 *"Ever since 1945 I have felt"*: letter from David Teale to his parents, January 12, 1945, Teale Papers, series III, box 146, folder 2950.

83 *"How taut and strange"*: JNWS, vol. 2, part 1, 78.

86 *"pattern blended perfectly with its background"*: NWS, 142.

86 *The story of Fripp Island*: see Miller 2006.

Chapter 8. The Next Generation

89 *"swamp without standing water"*: NWS, 246.

91 *"The isolated shore that had remained"*: NWS, 252.

91 *"like a long city"*: JNWS, vol. 1, part 3, 189.

91 *"Nowhere else in our travels"*: NWS, 252.

92 *"An aspiring nature writer"*: Teale, "Adventures in Making a Living," 3:74.

92 *"filled with contagious enthusiasm"*: Terres, x.

94 *"methods known to hunters"*: Terres, xix.

94 *"ball of dry vegetation"*: NWS, 129.

94 *he not only captured his first golden mouse*: Terres, 130.

95 *"receiving letters from home"*: H. W. Harris, 17.

96 *"acknowledging past human impacts"*: Cronon, 37.

96 *"When we choose the kind of nature"*: MacKinnon, 141.

Chapter 9. The Prettiest Shade of Red

99 *"haunted with a vision"* and following: Hawthorne, 45.

101 *"pink with red dust"*: NWS, 165.

102 *"lofty stacks"*: NWS, 167.

103 *"this moonscape"*: NWS, 167.

104 *When he placed a thermometer beside the anthill*: NWS, 166.

106 *"calendars are meaningless"*: NWS, 151.

106 *"wheeling forms"*: NWS, 154.

106   "metallic, grating, high-pitched": NWS, 155.

107   "Today, amphibians enjoy the dubious distinction": Kolbert, 17.

107   "during any given twenty-four hour period": Kolbert, 198.

107   "heating associated with a doubling of CO_2": Nicholson 320.

108   "cloud condensation nuclei": Goodell, 169.

108   "to completely compensate for a doubling": John Latham qtd. in Goodell, 174.

108   "feasibility does not necessarily mean" and "reduce the planet's fever": Nicholson, 325.

Chapter 10. Atop Clingmans Dome

109   "walking into a cathedral": Camuto, 227.

110   "The woods had a different look": Camuto, 293.

110   "I extend my arms": Thurmond ms.

110   "Nothing in the world is more alive": NWS, 177.

110   "Myrtles, magnolias, Maryland yellowthroats": NWS, 179.

111   "You need to be out in nature": Rosen, 8.

111   "It's a funny river": Bass, 139.

112   "the equivalent of moving backward": NWS, 184.

112   "home to the richest flora": NWS, 189.

112   "bleak as bones": Camuto, 217.

114   "raised their cameras, tablets, and phones": Hanson, 58.

114   "We should ban the use of drones": Hanson, 63.

115   "suspended animation": JNWS, vol. 1, part 3, 65.

116   "museum of the managed American countryside": Jim Morrison, http://www.smithsonianmag.com/history/75-years-of-the-blue-ridge-parkway-61889786/.

116   "It is the first use of the parkway idea": Jim Morrison, http://www.smithsonianmag.com/history/75-years-of-the-blue-ridge-parkway-61889786/.

116   Even Bill Bryson: Bryson, 95.

116   "By now we could close our eyes": NWS, 272.

Chapter 11. Jefferson's Phoebe

118   "A robin had built its nest": JNWS, vol. 1, part 3, 206.

118   "I am an explorer then": Dillard, 12.

119   "couldn't live without": Dillard, 168.

119   "There is always an enormous temptation": Dillard, 268.

119   Teale, true to form: letter from Edwin Teale to Farida Wiley, September 8, 1974, Teale Papers, box 146, folder 2829.

120   "The future is the light": Dillard, 101.

120   "Big trees stir memories": Dillard, 99.

121   "In a rush of such pure energy": Dillard, 192.

121   *"I preserve the illusion"*: Dillard, 75.

123   *"how many phoebe generations"*: JNWS, vol. 1, part 3, 206.

123   *"the lettuce bird"*: NWS, 265.

123   *"March 29, 1774 peach trees in bloom"* and following: Jefferson.

124   *"the author of the Declaration"*: NWS, 267.

124   *"four per cent per annum"*: *Smithsonian Magazine*, February 2013.

125   *"perfect house in a perfect setting"*: JNWS, vol. 1, book 3, 205.

126   *"some species of birds respond"*: Seidl, *Early Spring*, 96.

126   *"the genetic capacity to alter their phenology"*: Seidl, *Early Spring*, 96.

126   *"simultaneous changes in prey"* and following: Seidl, *Early Spring*, 97–98.

126   *"species out of sync"*: Seidl, *Finding Higher Ground*, 50.

Chapter 12. The Great Songbird Swamp

128   *"only sparsely inhabited"*: NWS, 254.

129   *"a great fire in prehistoric times"*: JNWS, vol. 1, part 3, 197.

129   *"the teeming wildlife we had expected"*: NWS, 254.

130   *"solidly massed banks"*: JNWS, vol. 1, part 3, 194.

131   *"plants with strange names"*: NWS, 168.

131   *"flat, black, and as large as dinner plates"*: NWS, 256.

131   *"a fleeting glimpse"*: JNWS, vol. 1, part 3, 195.

132   *"narrow-gauge track"*: NWS, 258.

132   *"hand-operated wheel"*: NWS, 258.

134   this *"Great Songbird Swamp"*: naturalist Brooke Meanley, qtd. in Simpson, 141.

134   *"mystery of the tip-ups"*: NWS, 257.

134   *"may aid a bird in acquiring visual information"*: Casperson, 31.

134   *"an almost eerie sight"*: NWS, 263.

Chapter 13. Saving the Pinelands

136   *"more familiar surroundings"*: JNWS, vol. 2, part 1, 45.

136   *"in traveling north"*: JNWS, vol. 2, part 1, 51.

136   *"wave of bitter sadness"*: JNWS, vol. 2, part 1, 49.

137   *"spring comes with especial beauty"* and *"barrens or dunes or tarns"*: NWS, 275.

137   *"the pineys began to fear"*: McPhee, 42.

139   *"a lake seventy-five feet deep"*: McPhee, 14.

139   *"generally stopped the march of natural succession"*: McPhee, 119.

140   *"tolerant, with an attractive spirit"* and *"generously shared"*: McPhee, 58.

140   *"where our footfalls"* and *"sang one of the oldest songs"*: NWS, 275.

140   *"alighting on the rough bark"*: NWS, 275.

141   *"first new butterfly discovered"*: NWS, 280.

141   *"ancient song of spring"*: NWS, 281.

142   *"four times as large"*: McPhee, 149.

144   *Teale recorded his first Baltimore oriole*: JNWS, vol. 2, part 2, 150.

145   *"the most beautiful of our batrachian sounds"*: Teale, *A Walk through the Year*, 61.

146   *"How strange a thing"*: JNWS, vol. 2, part 1, 55.

146   *"the quilted mountainside fields beyond"*: JNWS, vol. 2, part 2, 52.

Chapter 14. The Stuff of Legend

148   *"A great ocean beach"*: Beston, 2.

149   *"wild and rank"*: Thoreau, *Cape Cod*, 183.

149   *"mystery of the far-away"*: Teale, *Dune Boy*, 3.

149   *"Lilliputian flora"*: JNWS, vol. 2, part 1, 72.

149   *"gem of a small pond,"* JNWS, vol. 2, part 1, 70.

150   *"two harbor seals"*: Hay, 101.

150   *"a school of dolphins"*: Finch, *Outlands*, 48.

151   *"He came in a big, rawboned man"*: Teale, "Adventures in Making a Living, 1941–1951," October 15, 1948, 3:179–80.

151   *"Behind me, in my footprints"*: Beston, 180.

151   *"huge porcelain eyes"*: Beston, 181.

152   *"lobster lunch"*: JNWS, vol. 2, part 1, 68.

152   *"so singularly devoted to sucking money"*: Bryson, 153.

152   *"dreary peep of the piping plover,"*: Thoreau, *Cape Cod*, 71.

152   *"List of Birds Seen"*: JNWS, vol. 2, part 1, 147–52.

153   *"I thought as I lay there"*: Thoreau, *Cape Cod*, 172.

153   *"great rollers"*: JNWS, vol. 2, part 1, 67.

154   *"great number of windows"*: Thoreau, *Cape Cod*, 173.

154   *"The biggest sensation on Cape Cod"*: USA Today, June 7, 2012, 1.

156   *"most notorious visitor"*: USA Today, June 7, 2012.

156   *"impeccable environmental decision"* and following: Finch, "A Cape Cod Notebook."

Chapter 15. From Deep Cut to Sudbury Meadow

158   *"a beautiful summer night"*: Thoreau, *Journal*, June 11, 1851, 2:235.

159   *"still comes with the age-old beauty"*: NWS, 304.

159   *"the spirit and history of Concord's past"*: JNWS, vol. 2, part 1, 78.

159   *"wasp chewing on a faded pasteboard legal notice"*: JNWS, vol. 2, part 1, 84.

159   *"like a partially opened pop bottle"*: NWS, 303.

159   *"fine rain pattering on the foliage"*: JNWS, vol. 2, part 1, 81.

159   *"pink and white bells of the blueberry bushes"*: JNWS, vol. 2, part 1, 82.

159   *"smell of engine grease"*: JNWS, vol. 2, part 1, 88.

159   *"smoke and tornado of wind"*: JNWS, vol. 2, part 1, 87.

160   *"singing the rich, contralto notes"*: JNWS, vol. 2, part 1, 80.

160   *"It always seems disillusioning"*: JNWS, vol. 2, part 1, 82.

198   *Notes to Pages 144–160*

161   *"He set greater woods on fire"*: JNWS, vol. 2, part 1, 83.

161   *"a primitive forest, of five hundred"*: Thoreau, *Journal*, vol. 12, October 15, 1859, 387.

161   *throngs of sightseers*: NWS, 303.

161   *"one hundred and sixteen beer cans"*: NWS, 303.

161   *"building imitation Coney Island beaches"*: Dodd, 47.

162   *"the nobler animals that have been exterminated"*: Thoreau, *Journal*, March 22, 1856, 8:220.

162   *"Highbush blueberry, a native shrub"*: Miller-Rushing and Primack, 334.

162   *"around half of the species"*: Primack, 39.

163   *"average arrival dates"*: Primack, 119.

163   *"will be to the advantage"*: Miller-Rushing and Primack, 338.

163   *"nations have recognized limits to growth"*: Primack, 214.

164   *"climate change is happening now"*: Primack, 227.

164   *"finishing the book is a kind of rounding out"*: Zwinger and Teale, 237.

Chapter 16. Lost Elms and Flooded Fields

165   *"bobolink fields with daisies"* and *"large New England elms"*: JNWS, vol. 2, part 1, 98.

165   *"twanging, metallic-string sound"*: JNWS, vol. 2, part 1, 115.

165   *causes for the bobolink's decline*: Teale, *A Walk*, 185.

165   *"the winged embodiment of the spirit"*: Burroughs, 110.

166   *"What the live oak is to the South"*: JNWS, vol. 2, part 1, 106.

166   *special beauty on moonlit nights*: Thoreau, *Journal*, July 2, 1850, 2:53.

167   *"we could find only four chicks"*: Gessner, *Return*, 24.

167   *"undernourished"* and *"characteristic of penny-pinching"*: JNWS, vol. 2, part 1, 113.

168   *"brimming brooks"*: NWS, 316.

168   *"We've built a new Eaarth"*: McKibben, 15.

169   *"rocking-horse flight"*: NWS, 322.

169   *"Because it is so brief"*: Elder, 190.

171   *"This bird never fails to speak"*: Thoreau, *Journal*, July 5, 1852, 4:190.

171   *Teale had called attention to its melodious notes*: NWS, 318.

171   *"'Far in the pillared dark'"*: Robert Frost, "Come In" (ca. 1942), lines 13–14.

Chapter 17. A Second Longest Day

173   *"What will be regarded"*: Carroll, *Self-Portrait*, 181.

175   *"half a century ago"*: NWS, 170.

175   *"type specimen" sanctuaries*: NWS, 170.

175   *"The spruce and fir and balsam"*: JNWS, vol. 2, part 1, 111.

175–176   *"a far-northern spring"*: NWS, 329.

176   *"across the level of the valley"*: JNWS, vol. 2, part 1, 122.

176 *"bank swallows sporting in the dusk"*: JNWS, vol. 2, part 1, 123.

176 *"short pulp-paper logs stranded"*: JNWS, vol. 2, part 1, 118.

176 *"the change felt like death"*: Rebecca Rule, "It Felt Like Death," in Harris, Dickerman, and Morgan, 94.

176 *"which functions like an apartment-house clothes line"*: JNWS, vol. 2, part 1, 130.

177 *"begin their matins"*: JNWS, vol. 2, part 2, 15.

177 *"would coincide with the advance"*: NWS, 322.

178 *"We see monarchs drifting aimlessly"*: NWS, 95.

178 *"tens of thousands of monarch butterflies"*: NWS, 96.

178 *"scarcely twenty acres"*: Urquhart, http://ngm.nationalgeographic.com /print/1976/08/monarch-butterflies/urquhart-text.

178 *"In the quietness of semi-dormancy"*: Urquhart.

179 *"unpleasant, fatiguing"*: JNWS, vol. 2, part 2, 17.

179 *"yellow birch grow almost up to timberline"*: JNWS, vol. 2, part 2, 18.

180 *The thrushes' numbers have declined*: International Bicknell's Thrush Conservation Group, 14.

180 *"I think that the top of Mount Washington"*: Thoreau, *Journal*, January 3, 1861, 14:305.

181 *"In the evening light"*: JNWS, vol. 2, part 2, 24.

182 *"east to Freeport"*: JNWS, vol. 2, part 2, 34.

182 *"nearly a hundred mile" delay*: NWS, 337.

Chapter 18. Blessed Trail Wood

184 *"Rubber flippers"*: Teale, *A Naturalist Buys an Old Farm*, 182–83.

184 *"Sitting under the apple trees"*: Teale, *A Naturalist Buys an Old Farm*, 244.

185 *"Always hereafter, on this Saturday in June"*: Teale, "Adventures in Making a Living, 1974–1980," 3.

185 *"A note to myself"*: Teale, "Adventures in Making a Living, 1974–1980," 9.

185 *"I feel him near all the time"*: Nellie Donovan Teale Journal, Teale papers, series II, box 139.

186 *"Right now, in the amazing moment"*: Kolbert, 268.

Sources

"1st Cape Cod Bear Captures Residents' Imaginations." *USA Today,* June 7, 2013.

Barringer, Felicity. "Climate Change Will Disrupt Half of North American Bird Species, Study Says." *New York Times,* September 8, 2014.

Bartram, William. *Travels of William Bartram.* New York: Dover, 1955.

Bass, Rick. *Wild to the Heart.* New York: W. W. Norton, 1987.

Beston, Henry. *The Outermost House: A Year of Life on the Great Beach of Cape Cod.* New York: Holt Paperbacks, 2003.

Bryan, Dana C. "Wakulla Timeline and Limpkin Summary." Unpublished document provided to author via e-mail communication with Bryan, March 15, 2012.

Bryson, Bill. *The Lost Continent: Travels in Small-Town America.* London: William Morrow, 2001.

Burroughs, John. *Birds and Poets.* 1877. New York: BiblioBazaar, 2009.

Camuto, Christopher. *Another Country: Journeying toward the Cherokee Mountains.* Athens: University of Georgia Press, 2000.

Carroll, David M. *Following the Water: A Hydromancer's Notebook.* Boston: Houghton Mifflin Harcourt, 2009.

———. *Self-Portrait with Turtles: A Memoir.* New York: Mariner Books, 2005.

Carson, Rachel. *Silent Spring.* Boston: Houghton Mifflin, 1962.

Casperson, Lee. "Head Movement and Vision in Underwater Feeding Birds." *Bird Behavior* 13 (1999): 31–46.

Chidester, Peter. "Edwin Way Teale's Healing Journey of *North with the Spring.*" Presented at 5th Conference of Nature and Environmental Writers, College and University Educators, June 10–13, 2008, Booth Harbor, Maine.

Cronon, William. "Riddle of Apostle Islands: How Do You Manage a Wilderness Full of Human Stories?" *Orion,* May–June 2003, 36–42.

Dillard, Annie. *Pilgrim at Tinker Creek*. New York: Harper's Magazine Press, 1974.

Dodd, Edward. *Of Nature, Time, and Teale: A Biographical Sketch of Edwin Way Teale*. New York: Dodd, Mead, 1960.

Douglas, Marjory Stoneman. *The Everglades: River of Grass*. Sarasota, Fla.: Pineapple Press, 1997.

Elder, John. *Reading the Mountains of Home*. Cambridge, Mass.: Harvard University Press, 1998.

Feldman, James. *A Storied Wilderness: Rewilding the Apostle Islands*. Seattle: University of Washington Press, 2011.

Finch, Robert. "A Cape Cod Notebook." WCAI public radio broadcast, June 10, 2012.

———. *Death of a Hornet, and Other Cape Cod Essays*. Washington, D.C.: Counterpoint, 2000.

———. *Outlands: Journeys to the Outer Edges of Cape Cod*. Boston: David Godine, 1986.

Florida Oceans and Coastal Council. "Climate Change and Sea Level Rise in Florida." Florida Oceans and Coastal Council Report, 2010.

"Florida Struggles to Overcome Threats to Fresh Water." *New York Times*, June 22, 2012.

Foreman, Bill. *Rewilding North America: A Vision for Conservation in the 21st Century*. Washington, D.C.: Island Press, 2004.

Frost, Robert. *The Poetry of Robert Frost*. New York: Henry Holt, 1969.

Gessner, David. *Return of the Osprey: A Season of Flight and Wonder*. New York: Ballantine Books, 2002.

———. *Sick of Nature*. Dartmouth, N.H.: Dartmouth College Press and University Press of New England, 2005.

Goodell, Jeff. *How to Cool the Planet: Geoengineering and the Audacious Quest to Fix Earth's Climate*. Boston: Houghton Mifflin Harcourt, 2010.

Hanson, Eric. "Boy and His Drone." *Outside Magazine*, March 2014.

Harper, Francis, and Delma Presley. *Okefinokee Album*. Athens: University of Georgia Press, 1981.

Harris, Henry William. "A Journey from Catawba to Mineola." 2009. Unpublished autobiography by author's father.

Harris, John R., Mike Dickerman, and Katherine Morgan, eds. *Beyond the Notches: Stories of Place in New Hampshire's North Country*. Littleton, N.H.: Bondcliff Books, 2011.

Hawthorne, Nathaniel. "My Visit to Niagara." *The Works of Nathaniel Hawthorne*. Vol. 12. New York: Houghton Mifflin, 1883.

Hay, John. *The Great Beach*. New York: W. W. Norton, 1980.

International Bicknell's Thrush Conservation Group. *A Conservation Action Plan for Bicknell's Thrush*. July 2010. http://www.fws.gov/migratory-

birds/currentbirdissues/management/FocalSpecies/Plans/BITH_Plan_
July2010.pdf.

Jefferson, Thomas. *Thomas Jefferson's Garden Book*. Edited by Edwin Morris
Betts. Charlottesville: University of Virginia Press, 2001.

Jordan, William. *Sunflower Forest: Ecological Restoration and the New Communion with Nature*. Berkeley: University of California Press, 2003.

Kolbert, Elizabeth. *The Sixth Extinction: An Unnatural History*. New York:
Picador, 2014.

Lanza, Michael. *Before They're Gone: A Family's Year-Long Quest to Explore
America's Most Endangered National Parks*. Boston: Beacon Press, 2012.

Levin, Ted. *Liquid Land: A Journey through the Florida Everglades*. Athens:
University of Georgia Press, 2003.

Livingston, John. *Rogue Primate: Exploration of Human Domestication*. To-
ronto: Key Porter Books, 1994.

Lopez, Barry. *Arctic Dreams*. New York: Bantam Books, 1986.

Lum, Kaimi Rose. "Bear Buzz Hits Outer Cape." *Provincetown Banner*, June
7, 2012.

Macfarlane, Robert. *The Old Ways: A Journey on Foot*. New York: Penguin,
2012.

———. *The Wild Places*. New York: Penguin, 2007.

MacKinnon, J. B. *The Once and Future World: Nature As It Was, As It Is, As It
Could Be*. Boston: Houghton Mifflin Harcourt, 2013.

McIver, Stuart B. *Death in the Everglades: The Murder of Guy Bradley, America's
First Martyr to Environmentalism*. Gainesville: University Press of Florida,
2003.

McKibben, Bill. *Eaarth: Making a Life on a Tough New Planet*. New York: St.
Martin's Griffin, 2011.

McPhee, John. *The Pine Barrens*. New York: Farrar, Straus and Giroux, 1968.

Miller, Page Putnam. *Fripp Island: A History*. Charleston, S.C.: History Press,
2006.

Miller-Rushing, Abraham J., and Richard B. Primack. "Global Warming and
Flowering Times in Thoreau's Concord: A Community Perspective." *Ecology* 89, no. 2 (February 2008): 332–41.

Mooallem, Jon. "American Hippopotamus." *Atavist* 32, December 17, 2013.

National Parks and Recreation Act of 1978, S. 791, Public Law 95-625, 95th
Cong. (1978).

Nicholson, Simon. "The Promises and Perils of Geoengineering." Chapter 29
in *Is Sustainability Still Possible?* Compiled by Worldwatch Organization.
Washington, D.C.: Island Press, 2013.

Ogden, Laura. *Swamplife: People, Gators, and Mangroves Entangled in the Everglades*. Minneapolis: University of Minnesota Press, 2011.

Okefenokee National Wildlife Refuge Narrative Report, January–April 1947.
Typescript.

Okefenokee National Wildlife Refuge Narrative Report, 1969. Typescript.

Okefenokee National Wildlife Refuge Narrative Report, 1975. Typescript.

Orlean, Susan. *The Orchid Thief: A True Story of Beauty and Obsession*. New York: Ballantine Books, 2000.

Paes de Barros, Deborah. "Driving That Highway to Consciousness: Late Twentieth-Century American Travel Literature." In *Cambridge Companion to American Travel Writing,* ed. Alfred Bendixen and J. Hamera, 228–43. London: Cambridge University Press, 2009.

Price, Jennifer. *Flight Maps: Adventures with Nature in Modern America*. New York: Basic Books, 1999.

Primack, Richard B. *Walden Warming: Climate Change Comes to Thoreau's Woods*. Chicago: University of Chicago Press, 2014.

Rawlings, Marjorie Kinnan. *Cross Creek*. New York: Simon and Schuster, 1942.

Ray, Janisse. *Ecology of a Cracker Childhood*. Minneapolis: Milkweed Press, 1999.

Rosen, Jonathan. *The Life of the Skies: Birding at the End of Nature*. New York: Farrar, Straus and Giroux, 2008.

Rugh, Susan Sessions. *Are We There Yet? The Golden Age of American Family Vacations*. Lawrence: University of Kansas Press, 2008.

Seidl, Amy. *Early Spring: An Ecologist and Her Children Wake to a Warming World*. Boston: Beacon Press, 2009.

———. *Finding Higher Ground: Adaptation in the Age of Warming*. Boston: Beacon Press, 2012.

Simpson, Bland. *The Great Dismal: A Carolinian's Swamp Memoir*. Chapel Hill: University of North Carolina Press, 1990.

Sullivan, Anne McCrary. *Ecology II: Throat Song from the Everglades*. Cincinnati: WordTech, 2009.

Teale, Edwin Way. "Adventures in Making a Living, 1941–51." Unpublished journals, 4 vols. Teale Papers, series II, box 113.

———. "Adventures in Making a Living, 1958–80." Unpublished journals, 5 vols. Teale Papers, series II, box 114.

———. "Adventures in Making a Living, 1974–80." Account of cancer diagnosis. Teale Papers, series II, box 127.

———. *Dune Boy*. New York: Dodd, Mead, 1943.

———. Edwin Way Teale Papers. Archives and Special Collections, Thomas J. Dodd Research Center, University of Connecticut Libraries, Storrs.

———. The Journal of *North with the Spring*. Vol. 1, parts 1–3. Teale Papers, series II, box 215.

———. The Journal of *North with the Spring*. Vol. 2, parts 1–2. Teale Papers, series II, box 215.

———. *A Naturalist Buys an Old Farm*. Storrs, Conn.: Bibliopola Press, 1974.

———. *North with the Spring*. New York: Dodd, Mead, 1951.

———. *A Walk through the Year*. New York: Dodd, Mead, 1978.

———. *Wandering through Winter: A Naturalist's 20,000-Mile Journey through the North American Winter*. New York: Dodd, Mead, 1970.

———, ed. *Green Treasury: A Journey through the World's Great Nature Writing*. New York: Dodd, Meade, 1952.

Teale, Nellie Donovan. "Nellie Teale's journal notes, 1980 December–1981 January." Edwin Way Teale Papers, series II, box 139, folder 2836.

Terres, John K. *From Laurel Hill to Siler's Bog: The Walking Adventures of a Naturalist*. New York: Alfred A. Knopf, 1969.

Thoreau, Henry David. *Cape Cod*. New York: W. W. Norton, 1951.

———. *The Journal of Henry David Thoreau*. 14 vols. Edited by Bradford Torrey and Francis Allen. New York: Dover, 1962.

Thurmond, Gerald. "Sacred Woods." Essay in Thurmond's collection of nature writings in progress, "New Southern Highlanders." Ms. in author's possession.

Turner, Jack. *The Abstract Wild*. Tucson: University of Arizona Press, 1996.

Urquhart, Fred. "Found at Last: The Monarch's Winter Home." *National Geographic* 150, no. 2 (August 1976): 160–73.

Weidensaul, Scott. *Return to Wild America: A Yearlong Search for the Continent's Natural Soul*. New York: North Point Press, 2006.

Zwinger, Ann, and Edwin Way Teale. *A Conscious Stillness: Two Naturalists on Thoreau's Rivers*. New York: Harper and Row, 1982.

Index

Page numbers in *italics* refer to illustrations.

Ding Darling Wildlife Refuge, 39
Dismal Swamp Lumber Company, 127
Dismal Swamp State Park, 128, 133–34
Dominick, Gayer, 75–76
Drones, 114
Dry-grass prairie ecosystem, 27
Ducktown, Tennessee, 100–106
Ducktown Basin Museum, 100–101, 104
Dune Boy (Teale), 6
Dutch elm disease, 166

Eagles, 25, 32, 144
Eastern Meadowlark, 165–66
Eastern Seaboard, 65, 75, 137
Eastham, Massachusetts, 151
Eco Pond, 14, 20
Edward Ball Lodge, 56–57, 57
Egrets, 14, 60
Elder, John, 145, 169–71
Elm trees, 166
Endangered species: amphibians, 107; eagles, 32; Everglades kites, 24; Florida panthers, 14; gopher tortoise, 55; loggerhead sea turtles, 79; piping plovers, 152; red wolf, 78, 110; spotted turtles, 175
Environmental movement: DDT ban, 166–67; educational centers, 71; Edwin Way Teale and, 97, 135; fracking and, 105–6; geoengineering and, 107–8; human and nature interactions, 96; Pine Barrens and, 141
Everglades City, 13, 19
Everglades Headwater National Wildlife Refuge, 27
Everglades National Park, 9, 11–16; Anhinga Trail, 9–10, 18; controlled fires, 28; feather trade,

15–16; Flamingo, 14, 16, 19; Hells Bay, 17–18; Kissimmee River, 25–27; Nine Mile Pond, 17; restoration projects, 22, 26–27; rise in sea level, 20–21; Tamiami Trail, 8–9, 14, 17; wildlife conservation, 27
Everglades snail kites, 24, 58
Everham, Win, 32–33, 36–37

Faber, Eberhart, 45
Fabyan House, 176
Fair Haven, Masschusetts, 158, 161
Feather trade, 15–17
Feeder Ditch, 131–32, 132
Finch, Robert, 1, 49, 150, 153–54, 156, 169
Fisher, James, 30
Fisk Quarry Preserve, 169
Fitch, Linda, 169
Flamingo, Florida, 14, 16, 19
Florida: alligators, 10–11, 26, 29–30, 39–40; aquifers, 50–51; canals, 22, 26; climate change, 50–51, 58; development of, 13, 17, 38–39, 50; eagles, 32; Everglades, 8–18, 22–30; land conservation, 27, 32, 34, 54–55, 60; map of travels, 20; natural springs, 51–56; nature sanctuaries, 55, 59; restoration projects, 26–27, 31, 49; rise in sea level, 20–21; tourism, 9, 12, 14, 39, 48, 53; water reservoirs, 51; wetlands, 11–12, 19, 26–27; wildlife conservation, 27, 39, 45–46
Florida Association of New York, 42
Florida Audubon, 31, 51
Florida Bay, 16
Florida gallinules, 25
Florida Oceans and Coastal Council, 20
Florida panthers, 14, 36
Foreman, Dave, 35

Stephen Foster State Park, 62
Strange Lives of Familiar Insects
   (Teale), 119
Stronk, John, 148, 153, 156
Stronk, Robin, 148
Sudbury Meadows, 164
Sudbury River, 164
Sugarcane industry, 28
Sullivan, Anne McCrary, 9, 11–13,
   17, 19
Summerhouse Pond, 30, 81
Sunflower Forest, The (Jordan), 34
Suwannee Canal Company, 68
Suwannee River, 53–55, 59
Swallows, 26
Swallowtail butterfly, 177
Swallow-tailed kites, 31–32, 60

Tamiami Trail, 8–9, 14, 17, 39–40
Taylor Slough, 9
Teale, David, 4, 82–83, 187
Teale, Edwin Way, 1–2, 4, 7–8, 17,
   93, 95–96, 102, 104, 121, 135–36;
   alligators, 29–30; birdwatching, 15, 23–25, 27–29, 32, 46,
   79–80, 144, 180, 183; Blue Ridge
   Parkway, 116; Bulls Island, 74–75,
   78–79; butterflies, 177–78; cancer
   diagnosis, 185; Cape Cod, 148–49,
   151–53; Charleston, 72–73;
   Clingmans Dome, 112; death of,
   185; Ducktown, 99–104; *Dune
   Boy*, 6; early life, 6; endangered
   species and, 175; environmental
   movement and, 97; Everglades,
   8; golden mouse, 94; gravestone, *186*, 186–87; Great Dismal
   Swamp, 127; Henry Beston and,
   151; John Burroughs and, 146;
   A Journey through the Year, 185;
   Lake Drummond, 129, 131–32;
   Lake Okeechobee, 22–24; loss

of son, 4, 23, 36–37, 81–83, 136;
   Marco Island, 40–41; Marjorie
   Kinnan Rawlings and, 46–47;
   marriage, 5; Monticello, 122–23;
   Nantahala National Forest,
   110–11; *A Naturalist Buys an Old
   Farm*, 184; Nickajack Cave, 106;
   North Carolina, 89; *North with
   the Spring*, 2, 4–6, 17, 30, 36–37,
   49, 70, 83, 93, 135, 145, 153, 165,
   171, 182–83; Okefenokee Swamp
   Park, 62, *63*, 66; Outer Banks,
   91; Pine Barrens, 140–41; Rachel
   Carson and, 151; reptiles and, 173;
   Sanibel Island, 38–39; seasonal
   scaffolding in writing, 121; Silver
   Springs, 51–52, *52*; *Strange Lives
   of Familiar Insects*, 119; Thoreau
   and, 158–59, 161, 164; *Thoughts on
   Thoreau*, 164; Trail Wood, 183–84;
   Vermont, 165–69, 171; Virginia,
   118; Wakulla Springs, 56–59;
   Walden Pond, 158–60; White
   Mountains, 175–77, 180–82
Teale, Nellie Donovan, 1, 4; birdwatching, 32, 79–80; death of Edwin, 185; gravestone, *186*, 186–87;
   Marjorie Kinnan Rawlings and,
   46; marriage, 5; Trail Wood, 183;
   travels north, 8–9, 40, 57–59, 66,
   74–75, 91, 106, 110–11, 116, 118,
   127, 129, 131–32, 136, 140, 148,
   152–53, 165, 182
Temperature increases: impact on
   aquifers, 50; impact on birds,
   126, 180; impact on flora, 162;
   insect pests and, 141, 168; spring
   averages, 73, 113. *See also* Climate
   change
Tennessee: Ducktown, 100–105;
   Nickajack Cave, 106–7; restoration projects, 104–5

JOHN R. HARRIS has served as executive director of the Monadnock Institute of Nature, Place, and Culture at Franklin Pierce University since 1996. He was editorial assistant for *Where the Mountain Stands Alone* and editor of *Beyond the Notches*. He also played an important role in the Reflections Oral History Project, which produced five films documenting places and events in the region's past. Dr. Harris teaches courses in nature writing, environmental thought, and regional history at Franklin Pierce University. He has lived in Westmoreland, New Hampshire, with his wife and three daughters since 1985.